"Michael Hidalgo is a gift—as a pasto., a ......ner, a leader. This is a book you can't afford to miss."

Margaret Feinberg, author of *Wonderstruck*

"In this wonderful book Michael Hidalgo reminds us that the gospel is good news! Through . . . winsome narrative, *Unlost* rehearses how our personal stories connect with God's story. Without sugarcoating our challenges, the book inspires hope and confidence in the relationship that God desires with us. This is a great book for anyone who wants to explore their connection with God or who needs to be reenergized spiritually."

Reggie McNeal, author of *Get Off Your Donkey! Help Somebody and Help Yourself*

"Michael Hidalgo, a pastor, father and writer, has created a delightful retelling of the old, old story of Jesus and his love. Fresh stories, clever metaphors and faithful retellings of biblical narratives inspire me to come back to God over and over again, expecting the warm embrace of the father toward the prodigal son. Vulnerable and honest stories from Hidalgo's life show me how God's love can enliven and sustain the journey of a modern believer. I would like to be unlost myself, and this book shows the way."

Jenell Paris, professor of anthropology at Messiah College, author of *The End of Sexual Identity*

"Michael Hidalgo puts a bright light on the pursuing heart of God. In *Unlost* he combines his own powerful storytelling and the biblical narrative to peel back the clichés and baggage that too often obscure the truth about our lostness and the amazing story of God's pursuit and love for every son and daughter of Adam."

Larry Osborne, author and pastor, North Coast Church, Vista, California

"*Unlost* is the kind of book everyone should read. Literally. Everyone. It's the message of the kingdom, the gospel, the Bible, the church and every person—all wrapped up into a very readable and inspiring book."

Carl Medearis, author of *Muslims, Christians and Jesus*

"For those who through grace have been found by God, *Unlost* takes us deeper into biblical history and our own to reveal how amazing this is.

Hidalgo's compassion and authenticity call to those who have yet to be found, 'Take heart, God is still looking for you.'"

Shayne Moore, author of *Refuse to Do Nothing*

"*Unlost* reminds us that when God pursues us, fear does not have the last word."

Rebekah Lyons, author of *Freefall to Fly*

"Michael's book is a much-needed reexamination and rearticulation of a topic many of us assume we understand: the gospel of Jesus Christ. Filled with stories, soaked in Scripture and really quite funny, this book deftly connects the announcement of this good news (evangelism) with the process of saying yes to the good news (discipleship)."

Mike Breen, author of *Building a Discipling Culture*

"Michael has a true talent for seeing an ancient problem in a very new and redemptive light. For millennia, humanity has worked from the pretext that we are able to 'find God.' Our 'lostness' has been demonstrated by an arrogance that has compounded the pain of our separation from God. With depth and humor, Michael helps us realize that God has not lost us, and when we allow him to, he embraces us. Not only can I enthusiastically recommend this book, but I commend my friend Michael Hidalgo to you as a man who has lived this story and loves God and his neighbors intensely."

Jim Liske, president and CEO, Prison Fellowship Ministries

"*Unlost* is a treasure map leading us to a hidden gem of truth—*we* are God's buried treasure, and his unceasing passion is to unearth every lost, broken and irretrievable ruin of our lives. In this deftly written book, Michael Hidalgo blends dynamic storytelling with biblical scholarship and pastoral wisdom—ultimately reminding us of why we call the gospel 'good news.'"

Michael John Cusick, LPC, author of *Surfing for God*

"*Unlost* is an extended meditation on the meaning of grace—a reality many of us sing about, but too few of us really enjoy. Michael Hidalgo writes as if he were your pastor and your best friend wrapped up in one."

Brian D. McLaren, author of *We Make the Road by Walking*

BEING FOUND BY THE **ONE** WE ARE LOOKING FOR

MICHAEL HIDALGO

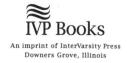

IVP Books

An imprint of InterVarsity Press
Downers Grove, Illinois

InterVarsity Press
P.O. Box 1400, Downers Grove, IL 60515-1426
World Wide Web: www.ivpress.com
Email: email@ivpress.com

InterVarsity Press® is the book-publishing division of InterVarsity Christian Fellowship/USA®, a
movement of students and faculty active on campus at hundreds of universities, colleges and schools of
nursing in the United States of America, and a member movement of the International Fellowship of
Evangelical Students. For information about local and regional activities, write Public Relations Dept.,
InterVarsity Christian Fellowship/USA, 6400 Schroeder Rd., P.O. Box 7895, Madison, WI 53707-7895,
or visit the IVCF website at www.intervarsity.org.

While all stories in this book are true, some names and identifying information in this book have been
changed to protect the privacy of the individuals involved.

Design: Cindy Kiple
Interior design: Beth Hagenberg

ISBN 978-0-8308-4415-9 (print)
ISBN 978-0-8308-8403-2 (digital)

Printed in the United States of America ∞

Library of Congress Cataloging-in-Publication Data
Hidalgo, Michael.
   Unlost : being found by the one we are looking for / Michael Hidalgo.
      pages cm
   Includes bibliographical references.
   ISBN 978-0-8308-4415-9 (pbk. : alk. paper)
   1. God (Christianity)—Love—Biblical teaching. 2. God
(Christianity)—Love. 3. Christian life. I. Title.
   BT140.H48 2014
   231—dc23
                                                              2013047717

P 22 21 20 19 18 17 16 15 14 13 12 11 10 9 8 7 6 5 4 3 2 1

Y 32 31 30 29 28 27 26 25 24 23 22 21 20 19 18 17 16 15 14

For Beth

You always knew . . .

Contents

Acknowledgments

Life and writing are collaborative efforts. Much love to those who have collaborated in my life and this book, especially:

Jay and Bumper, for not only being my big brothers but also the best of friends. Thanks for always cheering me on every step of the way. You've taught me more than you'll ever know.

Ed, for taking a risk on me when I was a young, unproven preacher. Rob, for helping me prepare my first sermon—and many more after that. Jim, for giving my family and me shelter during the storm.

The Gettings, Deugans, Warnes, Stockers and Lanes, for endlessly loving, caring for, and supporting my family and me. You give us glimpses into the way the world should be and, by God's grace, will be.

To "the guys," for reminding me every day that I am a beloved son.

The Denver Community Church family, for your constant display of compassion, grace, mercy, hope, justice and love. You teach me what it looks like to live in the ways of Jesus.

Brian Gray, Pamela VanderPool, Doug Paul, Steve Beren, Ryan Daugherty, Dave Neuhausel, Nick Elio, Amanda Pennington and Mike McFadden, for reading early drafts of the book and, most importantly, giving honest feedback.

My agent and friend, Greg Johnson, for telling me I can't be good at everything, and then teaching me to be good at something.

Cindy Bunch and the team at InterVarsity Press, for giving brilliant insights, passion and time toward making this book and its message all it could be.

Introduction

God Found Me

"Being a pastor is God's way of redeeming my incessant need to be the center of attention."

I found myself saying that to a seminary student over lunch a few weeks ago. He was grilling me with questions about what it is like to be a pastor: "How did God place a call on your life to serve in the local church? What is your daily routine? How do you intentionally model a Christian life for your congregation? What are the five best practices for preparing a sermon? How do you create space for your family amidst such a demanding job?"

With each question he asked I thought, I could, well, . . . lie. I could talk about how I wake up while it is still dark to spend hours in prayer. Or how I intentionally put my life on display because it is a shining example of what it means to passionately follow Jesus. Or I could speak toward my mastery of crafting a sermon. Or I could carefully explain the many ways I constantly and endlessly pursue being a wonderful husband and father. While it seemed that those were the kind of answers he wanted, I chose to be truthful about who I am. But the more honest I was, the more disappointed he was. With each response he realized that I am not a pastor who has all the answers to life's difficult questions, nor am I the perfect model of godliness he thought me to be. I am only a guy who experiences sin and grace every day.

There are many moments like this when I want to impress others rather than be honest. In those times, I am tempted to wander away from the love of God that does not need me to impress. And my wandering away is not just an everyday experience but it is the story of my life. Jesus told a story about a son who was a lot like this. Many call it "The Parable of the Prodigal Son."

As the well-known story goes, a son took his inheritance from his father, wandered off into a far country and spent all he had. After spending all his money, he hit bottom and got the only job available to him: feeding pigs. He was so hungry that the slop he fed the pigs looked appetizing.

It was then that he finally came to his senses, and realized his father's hired men lived better than he did. So he set off for home to apologize to his father and to ask to be hired as a worker. His plan never worked out.

When he was still a long way from home, his father saw him and his heart was stirred with grace, mercy and compassion. He took off running for his son, and when he got to him, he threw his arms around him, hugged him and kissed him.

In the midst of this, the son tried to apologize to his father, but he did not listen. His father interrupted and yelled to his servants. "My son is back! My son is back! He was dead and is alive again! He was lost and now is found! Let's party! He's alive!"

This picture of the loving father overwhelms me, which is why I often dwell on this story. In the corner of my office, between my bookshelf and a window, hangs a lithograph of Rembrandt's painting *The Return of the Prodigal Son.* I spend a lot of time staring at this painting. It reminds me that the picture Jesus created of a loving father is a true reflection of God, because at times, I still struggle to believe that.

The God I experienced most of my life was not like the father in Jesus' story. The father in my story stood at the door with an angry look as I approached with my head hanging low. He did not invite me in but kept me standing on the front step as he asked all sorts of questions about where I had been and what I had done. As I tried to explain what had happened, answer all the questions and say that I was sorry for what I had done, he crossed his arms tightly, sighed in disappointment and tapped his foot impatiently.

My picture of the father was created by years of seeing the way many in the church treated people who were like the prodigal son—people like me. Rather than forgive and welcome those who turned toward home, they punished and condemned them. These Christians frequently shot their wounded.

I grew up in a Christianized world. I always attended Christian schools, and after high school, I even went to a Bible school for a year before eventually going to a Christian college. All the while, I was never interested in what others thought I should do and not do. I never really saw myself as a bad kid, mind you. I was just a guy who enjoyed partying and all the things that came with that.

However, in my Christianized world, my way of life was considered horribly sinful. Many frequently let me know their opinion of my behavior—even if I didn't ask. I heard the judgmental way some spoke about my group of friends and me. Looking back it seems that the most judgmental people had never experienced the father's love for themselves, and since they had never experienced it, they simply couldn't give it.

But over time, this judgment and condemnation reinforced my belief that the father would never run and embrace someone like me. Anytime I was caught or admitted to my "sin," I was immediately punished. There was no embrace. It didn't take long for me to stop turning toward home—because who wants to go home to a father like that? So I wandered further.

The more I wandered, the more lost I became. I'm not sure where exactly I was, but I do know that I was a long way from home. Even still, as far as I wandered, something inside me could not let go of the idea that maybe if I did turn toward home God would run to me.

Like the son feeding pigs, where something in him knew the father would take him back—even if it was just as one of his hired men. I could not let go of the idea of grace, because as much as some in the church turned me off and pushed me away, there were others who were different.

These people acted much more like the father in Jesus' story. They did not seem to care what I had done. They only wanted me to experience the love of the father. As it turns out, many of these people had, at one time, been like the prodigal son in Jesus' parable too. Each one of them had wandered off and returned home to experience the loving embrace of the father. And once they'd experienced his love, they wanted everyone else to experience it too. It was their love, mercy and grace that eventually led me to take a risk, to turn toward home.

It was in that place that God found me.

I say "God found me" because we don't find God. Whenever a person says to my friend Scott, "Oh, so-and-so found Christ," he says, "Really? I didn't know Christ was lost." It is almost as though we think we have to go looking for the father when we get home.

The story of the prodigal son is the last of three stories Jesus tells in Luke 15. All three stories are about what's lost being found. The first story is about a lost sheep found by its shepherd. The second story is about a lost coin found by its owner. The last story is about the lost son who is found by his loving father.

How miserable would the story of the prodigal son be if he had to go looking for his dad? Imagine if Jesus concluded by saying, "And when the son came back home, he asked the servants for his father's whereabouts, and they told him he was working late and would not be home for some time." What a miserable picture: a son who has come home to find his father but who is left sitting on the front steps, waiting for him to get home from work.

That's horrid in comparison to the dad who runs and throws his arms around his son. Something about the way Jesus tells the story points to the fact that none of us find God. It's the father who sees the son "a long way off" before the son ever sees the dad. And once he sees his son, he hugs him and shouts, "He was lost and is found" (Luke 15:24).

All three stories in Luke 15 end with a massive party, think DJ, turntables, drinks, dancing, hands up, flashing lights and music thumping until the break of dawn. A party. Jesus' point in all three of these stories is the sheer joy of finding what is lost—not the joy of what is lost finding its way back.

The picture Jesus creates is the same picture of God we see throughout the Bible—a God who is looking for us. It's not about us doing all we can to get to God. The Bible is a story about God doing all he can to get to us.

This is what woke me up years ago, and it is something I am still waking up to. A few months ago, someone asked me when I became a Christian. I told them I've been *becoming* a Christian for a lot of years up until now.

Years ago I told God I believed he loved me, asked him to forgive me for participating in sin and confessed I needed him. My constant prayer since then has been, "God, I believe; help me in my unbelief" (see Mark 9:24). With each passing day, I know God's love more deeply. I've not yet arrived but continue to journey. I'm still learning to be honest with God. I'm learning to see that I did not find God all those years ago, but that the God I was searching for found me.

In this, I experience his love calling out to me as he patiently waits for me to respond. Love like this causes me to shed all the pretenses and the things I am not, because it wants to see—and wants me to see—who I really am. This is how love works. It does not ask us to change who we are; it asks us to stop being who we are not (see Greg Boyle, *Tattoos on the Heart*, p. 103).

I am not writing this book as a pastor who has all the answers to every question. I am writing as a beloved son who is in awe at the way God loves me. Because of this, each day I relearn the story of God, who is looking for me and for all of us. I have learned that the God we are searching for has been searching for us all along—and that's what this book is about.

My hope is that reading this will be another step in your journey, discovering the love of the father in the truth that you really are his beloved daughter or beloved son. May you see that you do not need to wear yourself out looking for God, because God is looking for you. And may your search for him lead you to the place where you are found.

A Couple of Couples

My wife texted and asked me to get a few things for dinner before I came home. I figured it would take five minutes. I stopped by our local market, quickly found the items my wife asked for, but then discovered only two checkout lanes were open. The lines for both lanes were long, populated by people who had shopping carts brimming with food.

I pretended to be patient, but inside, I complained about having to wait in line. *Why only have two lanes open at the busiest time of day? Is it that hard to schedule employee breaks?* Ten minutes later, still in line, I paused my impatient, inner monologue long enough to look at the magazine rack.

They had magazines on how to be happy, have better sex, lose weight, gain muscle, eat right, make money and be healthy. Other magazines were about the lives of people everyone recognizes but few actually have met. The cover that caught my attention had a picture of a couple known by one name, which was made up of their first names smashed together. The caption over the picture said, "DONE!" As I stared at the picture of the husband and wife, I did not want to read the gossip, know the details of the affair, or find out what she said to him or what he said about her. Something about the couple on the magazine reminded me of a young couple I met over ten years ago who, if famous, would have made headlines too.

◈

Ryan and Mya had just started dating when I met them. Though their relationship was new, it was as if they had known one another forever. Sometimes it seems like God has designed one person specifically to be with another, and that's how they were.

When I was with them, it always seemed like they were alone, but I never felt left out. Each was the perfect complement to the other. They could tell stories and finish each other's sentences without interrupting the other. Their stories made me laugh until my sides hurt. When they spoke of their life together, their dreams of the future and where they saw themselves years down the road, I was inspired. They were a matched set.

Over time, the subject of marriage crept into their conversations. No one who knew them was surprised; it only seemed right. They made the decision to head in that direction, and the only things left to make their future marriage official were a question, an answer, a ring and a wedding. Then, suddenly, everything fell apart.

Mya found out she was pregnant, and the baby was Ryan's. She called him and told him the news. He was silent on the other end of the phone for what seemed like forever, and he told her he did not sign up for a family. He hung up and never called back. Just like that, he was gone.

In the midst of her confusion and pain, she told her parents. Enraged, they refused to speak to her and kicked her out of their house. Her father told her she was an "embarrassment." Everyone left her. She had nowhere to live, nowhere to turn. Her future had just died.

A few days later I sat with her. She tried to speak between bitter sobs, saying, "I thought he loved me, but he didn't." Each time she said this, it was as if she had to convince herself Ryan really didn't love her and probably never did.

After sitting with Mya in my office, I thought of how often we think we have found what we've always wanted, but it fails to live up to expectations. For many of us, what we long for can be the very thing that wounds us. No matter how many times we experience this pain, we don't stop loving. With all of the risks involved in love, we keep going after it. We just can't help ourselves. The story of Ryan and Mya is far too familiar to many of us, but other couples tell a different story.

Amen.

Shortly after my wife and I celebrated six years of marriage, I met a couple named Len and Christine. Len asked how long I had been married, and I proudly announced we had been married six years. He smiled, tousled my hair and said, "That's nice." This would have felt condescending, except that when I met them, they had just celebrated seventy years of marriage. Even after seven decades they were still wild for each other.

Christine got around using a walker with little plastic skis on the front legs and tennis balls jammed onto the rear legs. She slid the walker along the ground as she shuffle-walked. Wherever she went, Len always walked gingerly beside her. In all the years I knew them, I never saw one without the other. When they sat next to each other, they always held the other's old, wrinkled hand.

They had been together for so long they did not need to say much anymore. Each knew what the other thought and what the other needed. They knew and they were known; everything was exposed. They had no fear, only total and complete love. They could tell each other "I love you deeply, more than you'll ever know" with only a glance. They loved everything about each other. He even thought her walker was sexy.

He discovered his greatest desire in her and loved her freely. She was someone who loved him for who he was, no matter what. They were a couple at peace. A few years after their seventieth anniversary, a friend called to tell me Len had passed away. In my heart

I knew Christine would soon pass away too. I got a phone call about her a few weeks later. She just couldn't live without him.

Two stories, two couples and two outcomes: one tragic, the other beautiful. Often we live our lives somewhere between those two stories, don't we? We want what the second couple had, but we live in a world where the story of the first couple seems to be all we can expect.

In their own way, these couples express the deepest longing of all people who have ever lived: the desire to be in the presence of someone who knows everything about us—the good and the bad— but would still die for us in the blink of an eye. We want love that goes far beyond shallow romance and will last when the waters of life become troubled. We desire love like the loyalty of a lifelong friend, like a mother with her newborn child or like a father who runs to us in a show of loving forgiveness. No matter how much we may want it, we quietly wonder if love like this is even possible.

Stories like the first couple have become so common many have been fooled into thinking real, lasting love may not actually exist. We are more familiar with hurt, betrayal and pain. While we may want to be loved, many of us have simply given up on the idea, thinking it's for someone else.

We want our story to be like the story of the second couple. We wonder if someone will shuffle alongside us and hold our wrinkled hand seventy years from now. Len and Christine's story is a picture of a love without conditions or demands, love that is not earned but freely given. The love she had for him was so pure, when he was gone she just couldn't live anymore. As wonderful as this is to dream about, it is hard to imagine this could ever be true.

But what if it is true?

What if we could be loved for exactly who we are? No more trying to earn love or feeling like we have to convince someone else we are worth loving. What if a love existed that was free of demands, manipulation or conditions? One story insists this kind of love is available, and the One behind this love is searching for you, for me and for everyone who has ever lived.

Some call this story "good news" or the "gospel." One gospel told of a child born a little over two thousand years ago. He went on to become a legendary king. Today, his name is instantly recognizable to almost everyone. In his day historians and poets hailed him as the "King of kings and Lord of lords," and he was called the "Son of God."

In a gospel written about his birth, he is called a savior for all of humankind because he brought peace to earth. The writer of this gospel claimed this news was glad tidings that came to all people. It was said our measurement for days, months and years should restart with his birth to honor him.

I am referring, of course, to Caesar Augustus. Were you thinking of someone else?

One particular gospel about Augustus celebrated his birthday. The good news was sent throughout the empire proclaiming that his birth was, for the universe, equal to the creation of the world. Many believed that Augustus was the one who would restore our world, which looked as though it was falling apart. The gospel goes on to say that Augustus was the perfect expression of human life and was sent by the gods to bring goodwill to the earth.

Augustus was not alone in having gospels written about him. Other Roman emperors had gospels written about them too. And news this good had to be told and retold. If you lived in a Roman city and were fortunate enough to receive a gospel, you and your fellow citizens would ask, "What should we do?"

You had to ask because a gospel changed everything—even the

way you responded had to be different. Gospels were gifts from the gods, informing citizens of a new reality, one that made the world better. This kind of news was always welcomed. Hearing it meant that now was the time to celebrate, call in sick, pop open the champagne, send up some fireworks and put on your dancing shoes. Who wouldn't welcome good news—not just back then but today as well?

We don't have to look far to find bad news. Media outlets inundate us with images of violence as a brutal dictator tries to hold on to power and quash rebellion. Television journalists tell of cities devastated by natural disasters, resulting in the deaths of thousands of people. We read about children who die every day from curable and preventable diseases, only because they were born into the wrong zip code. This brokenness is not just in other places in the world; it's in the cities, neighborhoods and places where we live too.

Most people would welcome a message telling us our world, our cities and our neighborhoods are changing for the better. Such a message would be called "good news" and may even be considered a gift from the gods. However, such a message *does* exist and is rooted in the God who is love.

The story is not about us finding him but about him finding us. His Gospel tells how the entire world—you and me, and all creation—is being put back together, bit by bit, one piece at a time. The Bible tells stories about Jesus going around preaching this gospel. He even told people in his hometown, in the words of the prophet Isaiah, that the Spirit of God was on him and anointed him to proclaim "good news to the poor . . . to proclaim freedom for the prisoners and recovery of sight for the blind, to set the oppressed free, to proclaim the year of the Lord's favor" (Luke 4:18-19).

Jesus often quoted the Hebrew prophets when speaking of the gospel. These prophets had spoken of God's promise to renew, restore, redeem and rebuild this broken world of ours. They spun rhymes and wrote poetry, lending imagination and hope to the downtrodden, oppressed and forgotten.

They painted a picture of all men and women sitting "under their own vine and under their own fig tree" (Micah 4:4). The prophets knew, one day, all people would be able to eat until they were full. I thought of this promise when I was in Mozambique holding a child who was dying of starvation, while his mother—also suffering from malnourishment—looked on lovingly but hopelessly. How good would this kind of news be for her?

The prophets told of coming peace in which empires and kingdoms would "beat their swords into plowshares and their spears into pruning hooks. Nation will not take up sword against nation, nor will they train for war anymore" (Isaiah 2:4). For every parent who has endured the loss of a son or daughter in a war, for those civilians who have been injured, been killed or lost loved ones because of bombs dropped on their homes, would this be good news?

The prophet Isaiah spoke of a day when there would never be "an infant who lives but a few days" (Isaiah 65:20). Years ago I sat with a couple whose son died three days after he was born. His mother tried for years to have a baby. She did, and seventy-two hours later, he passed away. I have never experienced a more agonized cry than that mother's. For her, Isaiah's promise would be amazing news.

We all need good news, and not only for our broken world but for our broken selves. Pain visits all people. The story of the first couple in this chapter is far too familiar for many of us, and we see it played out all over our world. We all have had the moments when, in our own way, we've cried and said, "I thought he loved me, but he didn't." In these moments, pieces inside us break. We need to know those broken pieces can be put back together.

The good news is they can be reassembled. Just as God is repairing the world in which we live, he wants to repair us too.

This is a message we all need to hear, and it needs to be told and retold again.

This message tells us that the story of the second couple is real, and a love like theirs is available. This is good news for everyone and everything—things in heaven and things on earth. This is what Jesus always seemed to be talking about. He said the good news is here and available now.

The promise the prophets spoke of was something present with Jesus and in him. His disciples did not miss it. Peter talked about it. John talked about it. Paul wrote about it. They understood the gospel was a message about the way the world would one day be, but they weren't so much pointing forward as they were pointing back. They talked about the way things used to be. They spoke of a time when things were perfect.

They knew of a time when there was no story like the first couple's, and when a story like the second couple's was the only one told. When we look around the world, we see glimpses of this time and this place that once was.

A few weeks ago I stood on a pier with my wife and kids, watching the sun set over the Pacific Ocean. I gazed at them: their skin glowing in the soft light of the setting sun, their hair blowing gently in the breeze, the smell of the sea in the air. Accompanying all of this was the rhythmic, calming sound of waves below us. Everything seemed right and good in this world. I saw things the way they should be, and was reminded of the beauty and perfection that once existed.

We see this in a mother gently kissing her newborn child. It is visible when you hike a mountain peak and take in the beautiful landscape below. You can even find it on your patio as you laugh, talk and enjoy being with your closest friends late into the night. These times remind us that, though the world is broken, there are moments when things are right. There are spaces in time when we don't see things as they are but as they should be—and by God's grace, one day will be. Through these windows, we can see what the world used to be when all was right, good and peaceful. A time that tells the story of a third couple in a place called *Delight*.

wow that's good

2

Naked in Delight

Try staring at yourself, as you stand completely naked in front of a full-length mirror. Seems a bit of an odd thing to write, but I am serious. I can tell you firsthand it is a tad frightening. I know because it happened to me.

My wife's great-aunt has a home in Southern California that has not been updated since 1974. The home has carpet on the walls, lime green and paisley-patterned couches, oversized floor lamps, and in the master bathroom tub, the faucet is a decorative golden swan (the water pours from its bill).

We vacationed there recently, and on the first night, as I brushed my teeth in the master bath, I looked up and saw sixty-seven reflections of myself. Every wall in the bathroom, from the carpet to the ceiling, is a mirror set at a different angle. It's a narcissist's dream.

You cannot do anything without seeing yourself everywhere. This was fine with me until the next day in the shower. I looked and saw hundreds of reflections of my naked body all over the place. The experience was a bit unsettling.

You may feel uncomfortable reading about the endless naked images of me that appeared while I was taking a shower under a golden swan, with water gushing from its beak, which should naturally raise the question, "Why are so many people weird about being naked?" For most of us, the idea of staring at our naked selves in a full-length mirror is uncomfortable to even think about. Add a golden swan to the equation, and it gets downright creepy.

Before we leave this thought, let's crank it up a notch. What if, as you stood naked before the full-length mirror, another person gazed at you in all your glory, but you felt no shame or embarrassment whatsoever? Hard to imagine, but that's the way things used to be.

The writer of Genesis tells the story of a couple who lived together in perfect harmony. No manipulation, deceit or insecurity existed between them. They "were both naked, and they felt no shame" (Genesis 2:25). This went beyond physical nakedness and spoke to the openness they had with one another. Nothing was covered up or hidden; rather everything was exposed. They were free to be themselves.

He did not have to act a certain way when she was around. She did not have to be careful about what she said. They were free to be open about everything they thought, felt and wanted. They were so comfortable and vulnerable with one another that they could stand completely naked in front of each other—with the lights on—and not feel a hint of embarrassment.

He never wondered if she was mad at him. She never worried about him finding her attractive. Their life together was a match made in heaven, created here on this earth. Not that heaven and earth were ever supposed to be separate.

We have been taught to think of heaven and earth as two separate and distinct realms, far from one another. Earth is our space. It's physical, something we can touch and see right in front of us. Heaven is God's space. It's spiritual, something out there, wherever *there* is. But this was not the way of thinking in the ancient mind.

Genesis 1 records God's creation of the physical world when the spiritual world (or heaven) already existed. The creation narrative then is the story about the moment when heaven and earth intersected and overlapped with one another. This is another way of saying creation is God's temple.

Temples were physical signs of divine presence on earth. They were considered to be the place where heaven and earth met. They were not just a place of worship but also the center of life. They served as banks, centers for education and, most importantly, the center of political power. A temple gave the king a platform for his role in the divine rule of the world. If a king built a temple, he was claiming a kingdom. This is seen in an ancient story about a king who lived in the Far East.

King Gudea ruled over the ancient Mesopotamian state of Lagash. He undertook the rebuilding of a temple called Eninnu. When the temple was finished, a statue of Gudea was placed in the temple. This only made sense since Gudea believed himself to be a god, and what temple could be complete without an image of god inside it? At the completion of the temple, Gudea and the citizens of Lagash dedicated the temple. The celebration and dedication lasted seven days. Six days of celebration and cleansing all led up to the climactic seventh day.

The primitive myth of the god Baal tells a similar story. Baal fought against Yam, the god of the sea, and against Mot, the god of the underworld, for seven days. At the end of his battle, a heavenly temple was built in his honor. An ancient poem records Baal's words when celebrating that he had built his temple of silver and gold. This myth was not just about Baal building a temple, but it was the story of how Baal became king and claimed a kingdom.

Which brings us back to the creation narrative found in Genesis 1. When God created the physical universe we inhabit, he created a physical place that intersected with his spiritual space. The writer of

Genesis told the story of God creating the heavens and the earth as though God built a temple. Creation was God's platform for his divine rule and reign in the universe. This is not just a story about how the universe formed; this is the story of God as a king over all creation.

In seven days he completed his temple, and it was good. The apex of his creation came on the sixth day, when God placed his image in the temple. The writer of Genesis tells us:

> God created mankind in his own image,
> in the image of God he created them;
> male and female he created them. (Genesis 1:27)

Up to this point, he had built the temple, but this man and woman were his image—they resembled him. I can't imagine how God felt when he formed the first man and the first woman and breathed life into them. I picture God staring in awe and wonder at a reflection of himself coming to life. www

⊕

In 2003, in the middle of the night when my wife was nine months pregnant, she woke me up and said, "My water broke." Like a good, confident, prepared husband, I groggily mumbled, "Are you sure?" We quickly grabbed our things and drove to the hospital. My wife labored through the night, and shortly after sunlight broke through the window in the delivery room, our first child was born, a son.

It was overwhelming, and when I threw my hands up and yelled, "It's a baby!" the medical staff looked at me curiously, as if to ask if I expected something else. My wife handed our son to me, this new life, so small, fragile and beautiful. As I took him in my arms, tears filled my eyes, and I laughed with joy and love. I knew my heart and soul would never be the same, and for that I was grateful.

We have had two daughters since my son's birth, and with each one, I stood amazed at the miracle, knowing I'd just met two of the most important people in my life for the first time. In seconds they had me wrapped around their tiny, little fingers. My heart was, and still is, mush.

Experiencing the birth of my children makes me wonder what God must have felt when he heard the first sounds of breathing and saw the first movements of life. I like to think he stood back smiling and laughing, with tears of joy streaming down his face. Not only were the man and the woman made in his image, but he loved them from the first breath he gave them. He simply couldn't feel any other way.

This God was like a loving father with his kids. He was like a parent coming home who is greeted by his kiddos jumping into his arms as he walks through the door. No fear or guilt or shame—only love and freedom and joy. The man and the woman met God and experienced him for who he is: love. Hardwired into their DNA as image bearers is the likeness of a loving, creative God.

It is no wonder that the impulse for love coursed through their veins from the moment God breathed into them the breath of life. Embedded in the first man and the first woman was the imprint of a loving God. They did not have to wonder why the other acted so nice or what the person really wanted. They loved without expecting or wanting something back, and they received love without thinking they had earned it.

They were free to be exactly who they were. They understood their truest and deepest identity as humans and were able to live in it unapologetically. God was not associated with fear or feelings of guilt, because they had nothing to hide. Everything was out in the open. Everywhere they turned, love found them, and in their freedom, they could receive it.

Together, they lived in a garden called Eden. *Eden* means "delight" or "pleasure." Eden was not just a dot on the map. If you visited, you would not have seen a sign saying, "Welcome to Eden. Population 2." Yet while you were there, you might have found yourself saying, "This is Eden," in the same way you might say, "This is paradise," while watching a sunset on the shores of Maui. Eden was not only a geographical location; it was also a way of describing the world and the way of life that existed in it.

In this place, God gave the man and woman authority, power and responsibility to work alongside him and preserve his work. God brought them to the Garden and said to "work it and take care of it" (Genesis 2:15). The Hebrew root word for "work" is *abad*. This is the same word used to describe the priests' work in the temple in Jerusalem. *Abad* was an act of worship. For the man and woman, work was a joy. It never felt like a grind or brought them stress like some jobs do today.

The man and woman worked with joy and anticipation, because they tapped into the purposes of God. In their work and in their care, they were able to participate in the ongoing process of creation with God. God entrusted them with his temple. From the beginning he was not interested in humans only living and benefitting from his creation. God invited the first man and the first woman into participating, working and caring for his creation alongside him.

In Denver, where I live, we have a large garden in the middle of the city. In the spring, when the flowers are in bloom, it is beautiful. The sweet smell of flowers fills the air, somehow keeping out the noise of the hustle and bustle in the city. You can find peace and solitude on any bench within its confines. I know many who love this garden and spend hours in it each week, because even today, gardens are wonderful places. Time moves slower, bees are not interested in stinging you, and the surroundings are breathtaking.

Yet as wonderful as the large garden in Denver is, the Garden of Eden speaks of something greater. It wasn't just about flowers and plants; rather, it spoke of food, contentedness, freedom and everyone having enough. A well-worked garden would produce food, wine and olive oil. It would give you everything you would ever need or want. What else could you call a world like this but "delight"?

Eden was more than the good life; it was the perfect life. If it sounds like heaven, perhaps that's because, in some ways, it was. It was the place where heaven and earth intersected and overlapped, God's temple.

You may be thinking that nothing this good would ever last, and if you were, then you would be right. This leads us to a tree in the Garden that had good fruit, because what other kind of fruit could there be in Eden?

what a picture paints this chapter

3

Denials, Leaves, Bushes and Lies

In the warm summer months of 1992, Guns N' Roses released "November Rain," a song that, although eight-plus minutes long and entirely too dramatic, proved to be a smash hit. The famous, whiny voice of Axl Rose, the lead singer, blared through speakers everywhere as he sang the lyric that reminded all who heard it that nothing in this world lasts forever. He was right: nothing does last forever. Most of the time we want to pretend this is not true.

This is why men and women spend billions of dollars every year on cosmetic surgery to make their faces tighter, their figures trimmer, certain things smaller and other things bigger. Try as they might, they're still just polishing brass on a sinking ship. Eventually, everything cracks, breaks, gets old, wears out and gets thrown away.

This is even more apparent with the best parts of life. The better something is, the quicker it seems to end—which is why middle school seems like an eternity and summer always flies by. So it was with Eden, the place of perfection. There are only a few verses in Genesis 2 to tell us about Eden before it's all over.

✛

One day a serpent questioned the woman about a particular tree's good fruit. This wasn't just any tree. This was the only tree in Eden that God had commanded the man and the woman not to eat from. He warned them that if they ate of it, they would die.

He challenged her, thinking about what God had said, who God was, and he blurred the meaning of what it meant to die. He pressed and tempted her until she "saw that the fruit of the tree was good for food and pleasing to the eye, and also desirable for gaining wisdom, she took some and ate it. She also gave some to her husband, who was with her" (Genesis 3:6). What was forbidden became the thing that was the most desirable.

We may like to think, if we were in the man and woman's place, things would have been different. Not true. We would have done the same thing if given the chance. In fact, modern psychology has pointed to the innate human instinct to want what we cannot have. Psychologists compare this impulse to being told not to think about something. The more we are told not to think about something, the more we think about it. The more we are told no, the more our desire is piqued.

My dad once found my Alice in Chains album, and when he found the album, he was so angry he tried to break it in half. As hard as he tried, the CD just kept bending. His fury only escalated. Not only did his youngest son listen to what he believed was trash, but he could not break the trash.

Needless to say, my parents were not fans of my music; in fact, they hated it. They were strict because they loved their children, and they wanted to keep us away from anything that might sully our minds. My dad bent a lot of my CDs in half in those days. Every time he tried to break one, it only made me want to go buy another. My response was more than simple rebellion. Something about not being able to listen to certain kinds of music made me desire to all the more.

This is how you or I would have felt about the forbidden fruit in the middle of the Garden. We could eat from any tree whenever we pleased, but not the Tree of the Knowledge of Good and Evil. Perhaps, over time we would have wondered what its fruit felt like, smelled like and tasted like. The more we would try to stop thinking about it, the more we would have thought about it and been tempted.

The man and the woman fell victim to this kind of temptation. They did the one thing they were told not to do, and it changed everything. They chose a path other than the path of life, love and freedom God had invited them on. Some call this dark path "sin" and those who choose it "sinners." *interesting def*

Richard Rohr defines sin as an attempt to find love apart from God (*From Wild Man to Wise Man*, p. 2). John Steinbeck points this out in his novel *East of Eden,* where he writes that "men want to be good and to be loved. Indeed, most of their vices are attempted short cuts to love" (p. 413). Sin is the lie telling us we can find pure, unconditional love apart from God.

The first lie the serpent told the woman was an attempt to lead her away from God's love. He said to her, "For God knows that when you eat from it your eyes will be opened, and you will be like God" (Genesis 3:5). If she could be like God, then she would not need him, and there would be no need to continue in relationship with him.

What she failed to realize was she already was like him. She was made in his image and had a relationship with him, the perfect source of love.

All of this changed the moment the man and the woman ate the fruit. For the first time, they saw they were naked. They felt things about themselves, each other and their world they had never felt before. Everything was different, and they knew it.

All their days in the Garden they lived openly with nothing to hide. They were naked when they worked, harvested, ate and when they lay down. Naked was normal and expected. Now they had to hide things that were open only moments before. They found fig leaves and sewed them together to cover up, and humanity has been sewing fig leaves together ever since.

The leaves hid their nakedness, but they were a lousy cover for the shame that now existed. They were still naked under the leaves, just as you and I are under our clothes. Like them, we are desperate to cover up. We don't want anyone to know how we really feel or to see what happened last night or to discover our dirty little secrets.

We all have spaces and places we would like to keep covered. But cover-ups don't work. No matter how much we put on, deep inside we know we are still naked. We may not want to wear more clothing, but who wants to be the only naked person in the room?

Many of us have looked at our naked selves in a full-length mirror and not liked what we saw. So we have convinced ourselves that leaves are the new naked. If everyone is sewing them together and wearing them, then it must be okay. Or, at best, this is just the way it is.

But this is not about the way it is. It is about the way it *should* be, which was the way it used to be, which is the way it will one day be again.

Once the man and the woman covered themselves, they heard the sound of God walking in the Garden. When they heard him they hid among the trees. God called out to the man. He responded, telling God he was afraid because he was naked. For the first time, fear is in the Garden. This is what humans do when we are afraid: we hide.

I hid from my dad once because I stole his new Volvo sedan when I was thirteen years old. *Stole* may be a harsh word to use, but it is what my mom always says, "Well, you know, Michael stole his father's car." She's prone to exaggeration.

What I really did was *borrow* the car without permission to go for a short drive. One spring afternoon I snagged the keys without my mom knowing. I went outside, unlocked the car, opened the door, sat behind the wheel, adjusted the seat, turned the key, slipped the shifter to "D," took my foot off the brake and stepped on the gas pedal.

I must have really stepped on the gas, because the car lurched forward, which made me lose my senses for a second. I took my foot off the gas and slammed on the brakes—except it wasn't the brakes, it was the gas pedal again. The engine responded quicker than I could compensate, and before I could say "dead kid walking," I was at a dead stop, with the passenger side of my dad's car crunched into a parked Jeep Wrangler. Did I mention this happened in my middle school parking lot in front of 200 of my classmates?

Students gathered around to look at the damage. They said things like, "Dude, you just wrecked your dad's car!" and, "Man, your dad is going to kill you!" In that moment, no one told me anything I did not already know. After all, I was there when the car crashed, and at times, my dad killing me seemed like an imminent possibility.

I took solace in the fact my dad was in San Francisco on business as the events of the Volvo scandal unraveled. Perhaps his being several thousand miles away would allow me to escape him killing me—for now. I backed the car up and off the Jeep, which did more damage. Then I turned the car off, and went inside the school building to find my mom, who was at a PTA meeting, to tell her what happened.

I took the confident approach, and told her about the accident as though it was the most normal thing imaginable. She stared at me in disbelief, saying nothing. This was not good, and I knew it. As I stared back, I imagined myself getting further away from her. It didn't work.

We walked outside, and she stood beside the car, still staring in disbelief. I still tried to imagine myself getting further away, and it still did not work. She finally said sharply, "Get in the car." As I opened the badly dented, scratched, damaged passenger-side door, it let out a horrible screeching sound of metal on metal. When I got in and shut the door, the side molding fell off. Things only got worse, which proved to foreshadow the drive home.

My mom talked at an elevated volume the entire way. She said, "You stole your dad's car?" Before I could respond to what sounded like a question, she answered it herself and said, "You stole your dad's car!" Then she walked through the details of what happened. She said, "You took the keys from my purse! You took them without my knowing!" To show what she thought of the event, she repeatedly said, "You wear the crown of stupidity!" She, like my friends, told me things I already knew; she was just yelling louder.

When the day my dad was to return home finally arrived, the sick feeling in my stomach grew worse with each passing hour. That evening I could barely eat dinner and could not imagine how outraged he would be when he saw what I did to his car. Toward the end of dinner I stretched and yawned, telling my mom I was really tired and needed to go to bed. It was 6:45 p.m.

I ran away, knowing that, at any moment, the man I called "Dad" would walk in the door of our home. So I went upstairs and pretended to fall asleep. When my dad finally arrived home, he came to my bedroom, opened the door, and said calmly but firmly, "We will talk about this tomorrow." The following day I learned of his plan for me to spend the summer working for him to pay off the damage I did to the car.

The night my dad came home, I didn't really go to bed. Rather, I hid because I was afraid. Thousands of years after the man and the woman hid from God, we find ourselves doing the same thing.

When God called out to the man, he replied, "I was afraid because I was naked; so I hid" (Genesis 3:10). But when the man and the woman heard God walking in the Garden, they were not naked. They had sewed fig leaves together to cover their nakedness, but they knew God saw through the fig leaves. No matter how much clothing they put on, he could still see what they tried to hide, and they were terrified.

The man and the woman looked through the lens of fear, which is tinted with shame and guilt. They were scared of the God who, when he created them, laughed with tears of joy streaming down his face. They were still in the Garden but a million miles from Eden. Everything became a frayed mess.

The world they lived in ruptured. Were I there with the man and the woman, I would have had a lot of questions for God. I like to think I would have asked, "Did you really have to put the tree there, in the middle of the Garden? Didn't you think that would have been a bit too tempting every day? Why not put it far away or perhaps not speak of its existence? Why take the risk?" Of course, I would have asked these questions while adjusting my fig leaves.

God's response to my questions would have spoken to the nature of love. For love to be true, there has to be choice. Love is, by its very nature, free, and freedom always allows for choice. This is the beauty of love, and it is something I discovered more than twenty years ago.

$\oplus$

I met a girl who came to our high school from California. We quickly became friends, and it did not take long before I was smitten with her. Over the next several years our friendship grew, and in college we began dating. Several months after our college graduation we went on a date, and I had a diamond ring in my pocket. We ate dinner together and then went for a walk to a bridge. Not just any bridge. It was the place where we first hung out years earlier. It was there that I took a risk and asked her to marry me.

I say that I took a risk because I was not forcing her to say yes. I did not demand she marry me. I did not brandish a weapon and threaten her. If I had done that, she may have said yes out of fear, but I would never have truly known if she wanted to marry me. Instead, when I asked her, she could have said no, but she didn't. She took a risk too. Love is a risk because it allows for freedom.

This is how it was for the couple in the Garden. They were free to choose God's path or the other path. They were free to eat from any tree in the Garden or to eat from the Tree of the Knowledge of Good and Evil. They sinned by choosing the latter, and their world blew to pieces.

Sin is messy business. It is never neat and clean. We would rather believe life is consequence-free. After all, who wants to clean up the shattered mess sin leaves behind? Maybe this is why talking about it has, for some, become more challenging. If I am honest, I am often a little hesitant to speak about sin.

While *sin* is a small word, it has been transformed into a massive weapon. A weapon used to divide, to belittle, to puff up and to dismiss many. When some speak of sin, the talk rarely begins with their own stuff. They speak about other people's sin. They call those other people "sinners."

Without even realizing it, many of us try to neatly categorize sin into the "great sins" and the "lesser sins." As these categories are created, we can label people like a can of soup, and put them on the right shelf. Identification becomes easy. What this kind of thinking fails to see is labeling and judging like this is itself sinful. Whenever we use sin to differentiate ourselves from anyone, we err.

So much talk about sin has been used to exclude. Most dialogue has devolved into monologue, and the subject of sin has become a soapbox for the self-righteous to stand on and preach hellfire and damnation to the wandering masses.

This is why I am often hesitant to speak about sin. Not because I do not think it exists, or because I want everyone to like me, or because it's not very trendy, or because I am a relativist, or even because of the fact that saying the word *sin* sounds punitive. The reason I do not like to talk much about sin is because of the way *sin* has often been used.

Regardless of how I, or anyone, feel about sin, the story of the Garden tells us that sin entered the world. It wrapped its long, dark fingers around the soul of humanity, refused to let go and is central to the story we find ourselves in today. Perhaps we need to become more serious about sin in our lives and in the world today.

Maybe the real problem is not only that we speak of sin incorrectly but also that we limit our understanding of it. Sin is far more than simple wrongdoing or a bad moral choice. Sin is the power of the kingdom of darkness that actively works against God's good creation. It is an oppressive force. It invites us to find love apart from God.

When we sin then, we participate with this power and agree to actively work against God's good creation. When the man and the woman chose to eat the fruit in the Garden, they gave their allegiance to the kingdom of darkness. In doing so, they agreed to participate in it and live according to its rules. Like the man and the woman, all of us participate in sin. Since the day they ate the fruit, humanity and all creation continually suffer beneath the crushing indignity of sin. This power is at war with the kingdom of God.

Our world is broken because of sin. Our world is broken because we resist the love of God and attempt to find love elsewhere. While many use talk of sin as a weapon, this is not a reason to walk away from the reality of it. We must walk into the messiness if we ever want to remove the leaves and come out of hiding.

Sin ruptured the relationship between the man and the woman, and between them and God. When they covered up and hid, they became isolated by fear and abandoned the freedom of love. This is not the design of God; this is the impact of sin. Sin isolates. The isolation begins with small things like fig leaves, but the loneliness grows. In our isolation and loneliness we attempt to find love apart from God. We do all we can to search for it, but we never will find it apart from God.

We might want to believe with Guns N' Roses that nothing lasts forever, but now, thousands of years later, we still carry so much shame and fear that we continue to hide. Too many times we root ourselves in this part of the story, telling ourselves we are nothing more than awful creatures that are beyond love. Thinking like this makes us wonder if God would ever think we were worth rescuing.

4

More Than Maggots

Have you ever had moments when you've felt overlooked or out of place? Times when you felt lost? It's the feeling you get when you walk into a room filled with people in the middle of a conversation, and someone says something like, "Let me guess, he used mustard?" When everyone bursts out laughing, you get the sense you've missed something.

This is how I felt most of my life growing up in the church. People spoke about God and others nodded their heads or got excited, but the whole church thing never made much sense to me. I heard of God's redemption and renewal of the world, and assumed I'd be overlooked in the end. I never was able to locate myself in God's story and was sure he hadn't found me in it either. reminds me of ethan

My relationship with God, if you could call it that, was me trying to survive, which is why I spent so much time covering myself with leaves and hiding. Why wouldn't I? The prospect of God ever finding me was terrifying. He was an angry, sinister God who would surely judge me for the life I was living.

If I could just survive until the end, then perhaps he would begrudgingly welcome me into his kingdom. This is the idea of God I grew up with, and one I heard preached and yelled from pulpits from the time I was young. Even our church's youth group heard this message more than I care to remember.

When I was in high school, our youth group took winter weekend retreats every year. We traveled by bus to the snowy, frigid, northern reaches of Michigan to a camp that was a winter playground. We went tubing, skiing, snowshoeing, had snowball fights, ice-skated and played hockey. During these retreats we had to go to several meetings. What I remember most is not the skits, the contests or the songs. What will be forever seared into my mind was the ear-splitting volume. Our youth pastor had an undiagnosed addiction to sound systems and microphones, and he always cranked the volume up to dangerous levels.

One particular retreat we had a guest speaker for the weekend, and we had no idea what lay in store for us. The first few meetings were fine, but the final meeting was completely unexpected. He began by speaking softly and slowly. With each passing moment he grew more passionate, his voice grew louder, and he spoke faster until he yelled at a rapid pace. With the aid of the massive sound system, his voice sounded like God himself thundering in that small room.

He yelled about sin, told us what miserable creatures we were, how we deserved to burn, and how Jesus came to save us from hell. The crescendo of his sermon was when he yelled, "Do you realize what God did to save you? YOU ARE A MAGGOT! You're all maggots! Jesus became a maggot for you! But you reject him! Do you know where God sends maggots who reject him?"

This probably wasn't the best thing to say, especially to a freshman in high school like me who was racked with self-esteem issues. I was barely five feet tall, weighed less than one hundred pounds, and was frantically knocking on the door of puberty—only to find, time and again, there was no answer. Now some preacher yelled at me about being a maggot.

What he didn't know was I already thought I was a maggot. That was why I was hiding. I knew exactly what God did to maggots. The larger problem was I wasn't the only one in the room who felt that way. It's no different today. People everywhere believe the same thing about themselves too.

very true

Believing we are not good enough seems to be a part of the human condition. It's called shame, and we are racked with it. So many of us tell ourselves we are not enough. We believe if someone finds out who we really are, they will not accept us or desire us. We hold tightly to a fear of rejection, and this fear keeps us in hiding.

This experience is what God described to the man and the woman in Genesis 3. He told them what life would be like after choosing a path other than his. In that moment, humanity was saddled with the lie that constantly tells us we are never enough. This lie plagues everyone at one time or another because we are conditioned by shame. Nearly everything we think, say and do is tinged with fear, which is why so many live every day only trying to prove their worth. We do all we can to appear perfect, and when our imperfection is exposed, we melt.

We have a miserable awareness of not being who we are supposed to be and never measuring up to others' unachievable expectations. We listen to the voices telling us we are worthless and unlovable, and what's worse is that we believe them. These voices don't come right out and say, "You are worthless and unlovable." No, they are subtler.

We hear them when we see images on magazines of perfect, sculpted, flawless, beautiful people. We compare ourselves to them, and it becomes obvious we don't measure up. We hear them when we get overlooked for a promotion at work—again. We tell ourselves we don't have the talent to get the next opportunity. We hear them when she breaks up with us, or when he says, "It's not you, it's me." What we really hear is that someone we desire no longer desires us. We begin to wonder if we are desirable at all.

These experiences are soul crushing.

As a result we tell ourselves we won't ever get into a position where someone can reject us again. Then we do, and we get rejected again. In those moments, we wonder why we keep getting our hopes up only to be let down again.

After a while the risk, the rejection and the pain get tiring, so we hold others at a distance. If they get too close, they will be in a place to hurt us. Once we know the pain of rejection, we do all we can to make sure we don't fall victim again. In the moments when we are afraid of being hurt, used or rejected again, we cover up and hide a little more.

This fear colors the way we see our world. Fear is so normal we wouldn't know what to do if we were not scared of something. Too often, shame has become our guide in life, whispering to us that we are worthless. We believe if we walk out and take off the leaves, we will be rejected because no one could want someone like us.

In the meeting on the last night of that retreat all those years ago, the guest speaker touched on a lie that has become far too popular. It suggests we are horrid individuals, and God finally decided to help us out of the mess we created. When we do this, we not only insult ourselves, we insult God too.

This is not good news. It's bad news in attractive packaging.

The guest speaker may have thought he had woken us up to our sin, but what he really said to God was, "You paid how much?" This is what you say to a person who buys a junk car for a lot of money. Everyone knows he got ripped off because the car isn't worth anywhere near what he paid.

My lifelong friend Kevin knows all about this. My sophomore year of high school Kevin called to tell me he bought a new car. He was so excited, and so was I. This car meant freedom. We could go anywhere together and not have to rely on our parents anymore. He headed over to my house immediately. He couldn't drive fast enough to get there.

Finally, after what seemed like hours, a car rolled down our street and pulled into our driveway. The original paint color was blue, but the car was so rusted out that the color was now brownish-red with blue accents. The fenders had holes in them large enough to throw a cat through, and the grille on the front of the car was missing. In addition, the muffler was falling off, so the sheer noise of the car shook the foundation of our house.

I wondered why this car was in our driveway, and then, to my astonishment, Kevin stepped out of the car. He was so proud of his purchase, but I was in disbelief. He told me he bought a "new" car, but the vehicle in my driveway wasn't new and barely qualified as a car.

I walked outside, and he proudly asked, "What do you think?" The car was a 1973 Toyota Celica he had named Tom. If my name was Tom I would have been deeply offended.

I looked at Tom and wanted to say, "This is awful. Please tell me someone paid you to take this off their hands." But he was so proud that I couldn't bring myself to say what I really thought. So I did what any best friend would do in that situation: I lied. I told him the car was awesome, and I wanted to go for a ride.

I climbed in and sat in the passenger seat. The seat springs poked into my thighs through the crumbling foam and shredded vinyl. I looked for a seat belt, but couldn't find it until Kevin explained that the seatbelt was behind the seat. I had to unscrew it, pull it over my waist and then screw the latch back in. He said, "Technically it's not legal, but it *should* hold up." I wondered if I had just forfeited my life.

He backed out of our driveway, and we drove away, yelling over the noise of the radio he had turned up to drown out the noise of the half-muffler. I asked him how much he paid for the car. He yelled back proudly, telling me he only paid $750.

Before I could stop myself, I blurted out, "You paid how much?" When I said this I not only insulted Kevin's car, I also insulted Kevin. I tried to lie again, telling him I was surprised he had gotten such a good deal. He didn't believe me. What I meant was obvious: the car was worthless and he had gotten ripped off. Kevin tried to explain all the reasons the car was worth the money, but even he knew he might have paid too much.

When we speak about others or ourselves as trash, we do the same thing. When we hang on to the lie that tells us we have no value, we ask God, "You paid how much? Don't you know who we are?"

Unfortunately this kind of thinking happens all the time. In churches across the world congregations sing the words, "Only a sinner, saved by grace!" The lyric to this song would be true if the Bible began in Genesis 3 when the man and the woman ate the fruit, but the writers forgot the first two chapters of Genesis. Those chapters tell of God forming the man and the woman in his image and likeness. This is our foundational identity. Like the song lyrics, many neglect the first two chapters of Genesis too. The more we ignore these chapters, the less we will understand the way God sees us.

His imprint is on every person who has ever lived, and he has given us a crown of glory and honor (see Psalm 8:5). We are meant to shine like the glorious creatures we are. C. S. Lewis wrote of the reality of human glory saying, "There are no *ordinary* people. You have never talked to a mere mortal. . . . Next to the Blessed Sacrament itself, your neighbor is the holiest object presented to your senses" (*Weight of Glory*, p. 46). This reality is hard to see because, even as image bearers, we are continually oppressed by sin. When God sees this, it rips his heart out, because it's not easy to watch something beautiful being destroyed.

In 2011, Jay-Z and Kanye West released an album titled *Watch the Throne*. When these two came together to record an album, everyone expected something big. The hype surrounding the album was sky high. The anticipation only grew as rumors emerged about the video for the first single titled "Otis."

Spike Jonze directed the video, and all anyone heard was they were doing something big. No one was disappointed. The video featured a Maybach 57, which is a luxury sedan costing around $300,000. They are beautiful cars and have every feature you could imagine—and many more you would never think to imagine. The video shows Jay-Z and Kanye giving the Maybach a bit of a makeover, if you could call it that. What they really did was tear the car apart using reciprocating saws, blowtorches and crowbars. Then they welded it back together and made something that looked like a car from an old apocalyptic film. If a car enthusiast watched this video, he would be sick at the destruction of this fine automobile.

My friend Matt is a lover of expensive cars. I have seen him look at expensive cars with the same love a mother has for her newborn child. People like him know what cars like Maybachs are worth and why they are worth so much. In a way most cannot understand, watching a Maybach 57 get torn apart makes them nauseous.

But people like Matt would not feel the same way if Jay-Z and Kanye made a video showing Kevin's 1973 Toyota Celica getting torn apart. Seeing this would not be difficult at all because watching something worthless get destroyed matters little. But when it's something valuable, then it's a different story.

As image bearers, we possess infinite worth. That is true of you and me and every human being who has ever lived. There is beauty in being human. There is splendor in skin and bone. We can see this in the heart of God. Nowhere in the Bible does God ever regret sending his Son to become one of us, suffer with us, and to be broken and poured out for all of his creation. God seems to think

Wow that is a really good point & beautiful

doing this is worth the cost. In the mind and heart of Jesus, the redemption of humanity was worth the price, and because of his gift, we are family, something he loves. This is not always the case with our earthly families.

My friend Dan told me about his nephew who is addicted to crystal meth. His addiction led to a life of crime, and he has spent the last several years of his life in and out of prison. During his first stint in prison, Dan was with his extended family during a holiday, and he noticed that no one acknowledged his nephew's absence. In fact, no one spoke about him at all. The shame and embarrassment felt by the family was tangible. But the way that family felt is foreign to the heart of God.

The Belgian, Catholic theologian Edward Schillebeeckx wrote, "If Jesus sat at your dining room table tonight with full knowledge of everything you are and are not; if he laid out your whole life-story, with hidden agenda and the dark desires unknown even to yourself, it would still be impossible to be saddened in his presence" (quoted in Brennan Manning, *A Glimpse of Jesus*, p. 205).

Some of us have done something we regret. No matter how hard we try, we cannot forgive ourselves for what we've done. We do all we can to forget, or cover up, because our greatest mistake causes all sorts of guilt and shame. We are terrified someone might find out, and if they ever did, they would never want to speak with us again. The reality is, Jesus knows, and he's not embarrassed to call us his brothers or sisters.

I recently met a fellow who spoke of never being able to measure up to his father's expectations. He has felt defeated all his life. Nothing he ever did was enough for his father. And there was a reason he never measured up. His father wanted him to be something he was not, and this was both liberating and painful. He was freed from his father's demands, but he also realized his father was not interested in who he really was.

Some of us grew up in a world where we were routinely told we were worthless. We were made to feel less than. Even though those words were spoken years ago, we still hold on to them, and as painful as they are, those lies still shape us. So we numb ourselves because we can't stand living every day knowing no one could possibly ever desire someone like us.

No matter how we feel about ourselves, the writer of Hebrews tells us Jesus feels differently. He wanted so badly for us to be a part of his family, to be liberated from slavery, that he didn't hesitate to become one of us and share in our humanity. He did this "so that by his death he might break the power of him who holds the power of death" (Hebrews 2:14).

How much do you have to love someone to suffer with them and die for them? How valuable would they have to be to you?

What if we held on to the truth that we are people of such worth that God could not stand to watch us suffer and die? What would it be like to see ourselves the way God sees us? How would we begin to see ourselves differently if we understood that we don't embarrass God? What would we see if we considered the fact that God has been pursuing us since the day we were born—because he thinks we're worth it?

Of course, we can come up with all sorts of objections to this kind of thinking. In my own life, I have found those objections are often ways of surviving and hiding. Old tapes play in my head, telling me I am a fraud, a loser and nothing but trouble. So I hide and do all I can to survive. But this story is not about surviving or hiding; it's about being found by the God we are searching for.

And if this is going to happen, we first have to know where we are. The problem is most of us have been told *where* we are and *what* we are. Like that night on the retreat, we have been told we are nothing more than maggots, and that we were on our way to hell. But God took a different approach.

Though the man and the woman hid from God, he couldn't stand the thought of being separated from them. When the man and woman were overcome with fear, covered themselves with leaves and hid among the bushes, God did not come to tell them where they were. He came to them and asked, "Where are you?" (Genesis 3:9). Because he came with a question, this means he wasn't only interested in speaking to the man and the woman, but he was also interested in *hearing* from them—really hearing from them. God is one who listens to us and doesn't just wait for his turn to talk.

His simple question demanded a difficult answer. This deep question tore away the leaves the man and woman used to cover their nakedness, and got to the truth of who they were and what they had done.

God's question struck a note of deep fear in them, so they lied, denied, blamed and claimed it wasn't really their fault. They were not concerned about what was true, but only with avoiding the question. Maybe this was the original sin. It started when the woman ignored the fact that she was already like God and continued when God came to the Garden.

Imagine if they had replied to God, "Well we wondered what the fruit tasted like, what it would be like to do it our way and not your way, so we ate it. Now we are in a big mess." They could have stated the truth, but instead they chose to blame and accuse the other. They continued hiding.

This reveals the difficulty in answering the question because it asks for complete honesty. When we read this story thousands of years later we, like the man and the woman, still deceive ourselves about what is true.

Most of us are scared to admit we have made a mistake, to say we have messed up, to reveal our brokenness or to acknowledge the darkness within us. Perhaps it will be of some encouragement to remember that everyone has messed up, made mistakes, experienced brokenness and discovered darkness within them.

The difference in people is not whether they are messed up; it's whether they are willing to admit it.

We are all at different places on our spiritual journeys. Some of us may have just experienced a heart-wrenching end to a relationship. Others may be racked with an addiction no one knows about, and it's slowly killing us a little bit each day. Still others are on top of the world, riding a wave of success, while some of us have just failed again and are starting to believe we have nothing to offer.

We have all experienced different pain: abuse, shame, guilt, doubt, illness, the loss of a loved one and the list could go on. Wherever we are, God is there too, and he's still asking, "Where are you?" This is his invitation for us to know him and ourselves. God asked the man and the woman the question; now it was a matter of whether they would answer truthfully.

But while the question takes a moment to ask, it takes a lifetime to answer. As difficult as this may seem, the confidence we have is that there is no wrong answer to the question, because we are where we are, which is the very place where God patiently waits for us.

We don't have to become a worthy person or strive to get to a new place to reach God. The spiritual journey is nothing like that. The real journey is the simple and challenging process of removing the leaves and coming out of hiding.

God did not stand far off from the man and the woman, demanding that they come to him—not then, not today. He is a God who is willing to come to where we are, so that he can invite us to where he is.

The good news is, wherever we are—no matter how miserable,

shameful, sinful or dark it is—God is there with us. This truth is found in Genesis 3, and it forever changes the way we see God. Just as God went looking for the man and the woman, he is looking for us too. He is doing all he can to get to us, and his question invites us into the truth of who we are and, most importantly, who he is.

This is what the man and the woman learned as they hid in the Garden, as they heard the question that invited them into new life. Unfortunately, they stayed in hiding, refusing to answer the question God asked, and as a result, the path they chose led them far from the Garden.

5

It's All Falling Apart

Sometimes I wish sin were as simple as a transaction. After all, we are all familiar with transactions. Nearly every day we pay for something, and what we get is in direct proportion to how much we give. A little money gets you a little, and a lot of money gets you a lot.

If every sin and punishment worked this way, life would be much easier. We could create a catalog to help us weigh the pleasure of sin with the agony of punishment. We'd be punished only a little for the small sins, while the really bad things would cost you. I attended a small, conservative, religiously affiliated college that attempted to treat sin this way.

The school built a subculture around rules. Their massive rulebook had rules about everything—rules about how students dressed, permissible music, where you could park your car, appropriate physical contact between the sexes, proper bedtime, hair length for men and women, and rules about how to obey the rules. All students agreed to live under these rules. In fact, agreeing to obey the rules was one of the rules.

The rulebook empowered the school administration, faculty, resident directors and students to manage the institution's preferred behavior well. If someone broke a rule, they could easily flip to a page in the book to find the exact offense and the corresponding punishment.

When hundreds of rules are in place like this, sin becomes simple. When you step over the boundary line, you are guilty and there is a defined punishment. This is what rules do; they make things easy for us. In a world like this, sin is simple.

If this is how real life was, then God could have shown up in the Garden, consulted his handbook, and pronounced his punishment on the man and the woman. Once they received their punishment, they could move on like nothing happened because their debt was paid in full. This would work perfectly—if only we lived in a transactional world.

But we don't. As humans we are not transactional; we are relational. We live in a connected, relational world. God created the man and the woman to be rooted and connected to himself, to one another and to his good creation. When sin entered the Garden, the fabric of their relationships tore apart. It's impossible to keep our sin from others. When something is wrong with one part of us, it affects all parts of our lives, including our relationships. The man and the woman learned this when they ate the fruit.

As they were about to find out, sin always grows, spreading in ways we cannot imagine. It's like spilling a glass of milk at the dinner table, a weekly event in my home. Even spilling a little bit in the bottom of the glass seems to find every crack and crevice in our table. The milk pours through the cracks, hits the hardwood floor and splatters everywhere. Cleaning up takes forever, and just when I think I am done, I find more in places I would never have thought to look—because milk defies the laws of physics.

Sin spreads into places we never think possible. There are times when we do something that seems like no big deal, only to have it blow up and affect everything. Many of us know the pain of watching those we love suffer because of our poor choices.

Last year I received a phone call from a good friend who was in a panic. He asked if we could meet right away. When we got together, he told me of his hidden addiction. No one knew anything about it. He made one small choice, which led to another worse choice, which led to an even worse choice, which led to many more poor choices. He thought he had his behavior under control. He told himself no one knew, his actions did not matter, nor did they affect anyone.

Then his wife caught him. She was devastated. She told him she needed space and asked him to leave the house for a while. He asked her how long, and she told him to "just get out." He told his daughter he would be gone for a while. No matter how he tried to explain things to her and comfort her, it was no use. For the first time, he saw how his sin damaged everything. This side of sin is rarely advertised.

The choice made by the first man and woman to eat the fruit may have seemed to be a small thing, but the bite of that fruit sent shockwaves into the world that we continue to experience today. Like the man and the woman, when something in us is broken, the way we relate to everyone and everything reflects that brokenness.

This is why sin causes pain, loss, anxiety, shame and mistrust. The results bubble up and spill over into places we never thought possible. Sin is messy. Taking a bite of the fruit couldn't stay between the man and the woman. They were relational, not transactional. God spoke to them about how far-reaching the impact of their choice would be.

God not only issued a punishment but also told them what sin would bring, now and forever. As a result of their choices, they would experience anxiety, sorrow and grief in all of their relationships until, at last, they would return to the dirt from which they came.

He told the woman her "pains in childbearing" would be severe and "with painful labor" she would give birth to children (Genesis

3:16). The Hebrew root for the word "pain" that the woman would experience is *atsab*. This pain does not speak toward physical agony, but toward anxiety, sorrow and grief. This was the new reality for all mothers to come. God said, "With sorrow and anxiety you will bring children into this world." How does that sound?

In her book *Raising Blaze*, Debra Ginsberg said having kids is like having your heart "bared, beating forever outside its chest" (p. 188). Something in the soul of a mother knows this in ways no one else can. A mom is forever knit to the child who grew in her womb. The reality for the first mother, and all mothers since, is the sorrow and anxiety that comes with giving birth.

The sorrow of the woman would be met with oppression from the man. God said her desire would be for her husband, but he would rule over her. Once they were equals working, living and giving love freely together. Now he would practice dominance over her. Since this moment in the Garden, women have been exploited, oppressed and objectified by men. Call it what you will—male chauvinism or sexism—this oppression is everywhere in our world.

A friend of mine was an elder at a church where they taught that only men could be ordained, serve as elders, teach or hold the title "pastor." Even if a woman had equal responsibilities as a man, she was paid less. Their reasoning for their viewpoint was rooted in Genesis 3:16. They taught that men should rule over women. Sin has gone so far out from Eden that we still see the impact everywhere today—even in our churches.

But God wasn't done. He also had words for the man.

When God formed the man from the dust of the ground, he put him in the Garden so he could "work it and take care of it" (Genesis 2:15). Now things would be different. God said to him, "Cursed is the ground because of you; through painful toil you will eat food from it all the days of your life" (Genesis 3:17). The Hebrew root for the words "painful toil" is also *atsab*. The very same thing the woman would experience in giving birth was the same thing the man would experience in his work.

In his words to the man, God concluded, "for dust you are and to dust you will return" (Genesis 3:19). In his attempt to be like God, he came face to face with his own mortality. All of this pain, sorrow, toil and anxiety would end in death. The man and the woman chose the path of death, fear and enslavement, and discovered, in that place, death has the last word.

Things did not just change after they ate the fruit: they went from bad to worse. Their relationship with God, one another and the earth was in shreds. They could not keep sin to themselves. Because they sinned, everything to which they related felt the impact. All of creation was marred by sorrow, grief and anxiety.

When they saw they were naked, they could not shake how uncomfortable it was for them. Maybe they wanted to open up to God again, but they felt this unexplained emotion that was new to them, called fear. No matter how they felt or what they wanted, they could never go back. Sorrow and anxiety were the new normal.

Every generation since has inherited *atsab* from the one before. Anxiety has become such a part of who we are as humans it influences nearly all we do. It has invaded all our relationships, even our relationship with God. Consider our religious devotion.

In the ancient world, people fretted over keeping the gods happy. They went to great lengths doing all they could to not anger the gods, and at the same time, they attempted to please and placate them. If they did this well enough, the gods would be happy with and may even bless them. Whole civilizations were built on this kind of thinking.

Nations had established civil religions with deep beliefs and mythologies about their gods. Many believed the gods were fierce and, if not pacified by the worshipers, would destroy the people. In the event something bad happened—famine, plague, natural disaster—

the people believed they must have done something to anger the gods. As a result, their worship would become more fervent and more passionate in the hopes that no further harm would come. Of course, with greater fervency and passion, anxiety grew.

Deep in the heart of every religious devotee was the lingering question, "What if this doesn't work?" If sacrifices were not enough, they'd be in for more sorrow. The prophets called this kind of religion "idolatry." No wonder Jeremiah used the word *atsab* to speak of worshiping idols (Jeremiah 44:19).

Idolatry is to entangle oneself in anxiety.

Have we progressed very far? So many still live bound to the weight of sorrow and worry in their relationship to God. How many times have we spoken with someone who makes a direct connection between their bad behavior and their unfortunate circumstances?

A few weeks ago I had lunch with a friend who has been married for six years and he and his wife have a son who just turned seven. They have experienced constant struggle in their marriage. He never got through the last few classes needed to get his college degree, and they have never reached their financial goals. Relationally, they have always been stressed, and her family is constantly putting pressure on him to do this or that. After recounting their marital struggles he said, "I think God is continuing to punish us for having sex before we got married." It turns out, he has thought about this every day throughout his six years of marriage. He believes God is angry with him and his wife, and their hardship in life is proof of that.

It's no surprise to know he struggles to attend church, doesn't want to read his Bible and finds prayer nearly impossible. No matter what he does, trying to right the wrongs of the past, guilt, shame and fear continually pummel him. This kind of religion tells him to watch out because God is after him.

This way of thinking is not just found in religion. In most areas of our lives, we live anxiously. Many of us have had trouble falling asleep the night before our annual review. We find ourselves constantly checking email every few minutes, hoping that that one message from that one person will finally land in our inbox. We anxiously wonder what others really think of us. Maybe you have found yourself hoping he or she will call you again—or maybe, never call you again.

We may think stress and worry is a normal part of life, but it started when the man and the woman ate the fruit. They saw they were naked, were afraid, and they hid. *Atsab* is the fear constantly asking, "What will happen if I come out of hiding?" Sadly, we have learned to survive by asking this question, and some have learned to thrive by using fear as a tool to get what they want.

Those who peddle fear are nothing more than pornographers. When people look at porn, they are stimulated, excited and aroused. Fear is not much different. It arouses emotions that raise our blood pressure and increase our heart rate. Over time we begin to crave this, and believe it is good and right and normal. We forget, however, that fear entered the heart of the man and the woman after they ate the fruit, not before. In God's ideal world, there is no fear, no shame and no anxiety. But we insist on hiding because we are afraid, and this way of living leaks into all aspects of our lives. We can't stop the leak—because we are relational, not transactional.

Adam and Eve's sin cut them off from everything, including Eden. God banished them from the Garden. They would not be able to rewind and get a do-over. They would always hide, feeling naked and afraid. They were introduced to a whole new world—one that was frayed, broken and torn.

In the damaging of their relationship with God, all relationships fell victim. When they ate the fruit, everything changed for the worse, but things were just starting to get bad. They had no idea how deeply sin scarred everything. Then they had two sons.

Their firstborn son they named Cain who, like his father, was a gardener. In gratitude to God he chose to worship him by offering some of the fruit he had grown. The younger son they named Abel; he was a shepherd. He recognized the sheep as a gift from God and, in his thankfulness, offered the firstborn from his flock.

When the two sons brought their offerings to God, he "looked with favor on Abel and his offering, but on Cain and his offering he did not look with favor" (Genesis 4:4-5). Cain's anger toward God and his brother burned within him. He asked Abel to go out to the fields with him, and then he attacked his brother and murdered him. Murder?

Just a few years earlier the world was described as paradise. It was a place with no striving, fear or shame. Yet one generation later, the man and the woman were left to bury their younger son who was killed by their older son.

I cannot imagine the deep regret the man and the woman experienced. How many times did they play the scene of eating the fruit over in their minds: *Maybe, if we had not eaten the fruit, our son would still be alive?* They learned sin always gets worse. The power of the kingdom of darkness does not stagnate but always grows.

God saw what Cain had done, went to him and, again, asked a question: "Where is your brother Abel?" (Genesis 4:9). Like his parents, he attempted to evade God's question, so he asked a question of his own: "Am I my brother's keeper?" (Genesis 4:9). His response to God reflected his self-centered condition and the brokenness that had come to human relationships.

To be a "keeper" of someone meant to protect him, care for him and, if need be, save his life. Cain dismissed any responsibility for his brother. His job was to look after himself and no one else. He had no concern for his brother's welfare.

God said to Cain, "What have you done? Listen! Your brother's blood cries out to me from the ground" (Genesis 4:10). God told Cain he would forever be a wanderer on the earth. Like a dead leaf blown about by the wind, he would be powerless to ever stop moving. Like his parents before him, Cain tried to cover things up—only to learn hiding doesn't work. He would live the rest of his years like a fugitive because sin never allows anyone to stand still.

His punishment overwhelmed him. Fear seized him and he was convinced he too would be killed. God vowed to avenge seven times over anyone who harmed Cain (Genesis 4:13-16). With that, Cain set off for a life on the run. As miserable as this story is, things were still getting worse.

Just a few generations later, Lamech, a descendant of Cain, bragged to his wives that he exacted revenge by murdering someone who injured him. In regard to his vengeful ways, he placed himself above God saying, "If Cain is avenged seven times, then Lamech seventy-seven times" (Genesis 4:24). In the days of Lamech the human condition bottomed out.

The description of the human heart spoke of how deeply people participate in the power of darkness. All humanity had become those who carefully crafted their sinful imagination. It was then that God saw "every inclination of the thoughts of the human heart was only evil all the time" (Genesis 6:5). The rabbis refer to this inclination in our hearts as our "evil impulse."

This impulse speaks toward the human tendency to selfishness, and this is no casual thing. The word used to describe the way we form our evil thoughts is the same word used to describe the way God formed the man from the dust of the ground—or how a potter forms clay on a wheel—something done with meticulous detail.

Our ability to form evil does not have to be taught, but grows inside us from the day we are born. Just watch children play together. Our family friends have a son who is a couple of months younger than my daughter. Before they turned two, they started fighting over toys. Their selfishness fuels their desire for the same toy. Typically, when one is triumphant, the other cries, and some form of revenge ensues. As they have learned to speak, they both yell at the other, "Mine!" We never really grow up; we just fight over things other than toys.

We do all we can to protect what is ours. Many have lost the ability and desire to share anything. We tell ourselves we deserve what we have, that we have earned the good life, and that we have worked hard for all we have. Our attitude reflects our arrogance. From the moment we are born we clench our fists together, grabbing whatever we can. We only open our hands and let go when we die. This way of living is seated deeply in the human heart.

We craft this evil with precision, like an artist giving attention to every detail. Selfishness has become the artwork of our hearts. God saw what occupied the hearts of all people, and what he saw there told the story of how they lived all the time. In their attempt to find love apart from God, they moved further away from his love and grace. The result was the desecration of God's temple; his creation was corrupt and filled with violence. What would God do? The short answer is, he would cleanse his temple. God had a plan, and it involved a man named Noah.

6

Everything Changes, and
Everything Stays the Same

I have had conversations with many people who struggle with the God of the Bible. Many point to several stories in the Bible as evidence of him being an angry, violent, judgmental deity. It's not hard to see their point, especially when they bring up the story of Noah. The story of the flood is a sickening account of God's destruction of humanity. He definitely sounds like a God who is angry.

But what would we think of a God who gazed on the worst kind of human evil and did nothing? Is that a picture of a loving and just God? We may not like the idea of God's wrath, but sometimes we want to see punishment handed out. We want justice to be served. This longing for justice, to see things made right, is also deep inside us; it's part of being made in the image and likeness of a just God.

The psalmist tells us that what is right and just is the foundation of God's rule (Psalm 89:14). As such, he cannot tolerate injustice. Justice is not about the way things are but the way things should be. It is about making things right, which means the things that are wrong have to be done away with or corrected. At times, God's justice demands his wrath, which is an outworking of love. ✗✗

If God does not rage against racism, sexism, rape, child abuse or "the arrogance that allows people to exploit, bomb, bully and enslave one another," then we can safely assume he is not a loving God (N. T. Wright, "The Cross and the Caricatures," 2007, www .fulcrum-anglican.org.uk/news/2007/20070423wright.cfm?doc=205). God hates seeing this, and he should do all he can to remove these things from his good creation. And that is exactly what God did.

Creation, God's temple, had been desecrated. In those days a man named Noah walked faithfully with God, as did his sons Ham, Shem and Japheth. Their lives were in stark contrast to the rest of the violent people on earth. Because of this God came to Noah and said, "I am going to put an end to all people, for the earth is filled with violence because of them. I am surely going to destroy both them and the earth" (Genesis 6:13). God chose to judge the world with a flood.

One has to wonder what was going on in the mind and heart of God when he decided to do this. We may be tempted to think he was filled with rage, or perhaps he threw a fit because things did not go his way. This is a picture of God many possess—and for good reason: it's what we've been told.

There was a time I was told, "You better watch out, Michael. You are in God's hands, and he is angry with you." The comment was intended to terrify me, as I had learned over the years what God did to people like me, and it was quite unsettling. As much as the hope was that this comment would turn me toward God, it actually drove me further away. In my mind, I needed to be saved, not so much from my sin, but from this God who was out to get me.

Looking back, I wonder how I may have thought differently if I had known that God's first response when he saw the mess humanity has gotten itself into was not anger but brokenness, sorrow, grief and sadness. His heart broke at the sight of his creation and those fashioned in his image being destroyed by the ugliness of sin.

The Hebrew word used to express his grief is *atsab*. This is exactly what the man and the woman felt when they sinned. God bore sorrow alongside humanity. He allowed himself to experience the same sorrow that the man and woman experienced as a result of sin. From the very beginning, we see a God who is with us in our pain—not one who stands apart from it. We are so accustomed to the picture of God sitting somewhere up in the sky, angrily tossing lightning bolts at us, but this is not what the writer of Genesis describes.

God's first response to the evil in the hearts of humans is grief and sorrow. He is a God who hurts when we hurt, and knows the pain we are going through. In *The Prophets,* Abraham Joshua Heschel points out, "There is sorrow in [God's] anger" (p. 83), which raises the question: What kind of God allows his heart to be broken by the actions of mere mortals?

In the ancient, primitive world, gods had little concern for people, but now we see the God of the Bible showing his heart by feeling sorrow and grief alongside humanity. This was revolutionary then, and it still is for us today. He is not just an ornery God up in the sky, waiting to make our lives miserable. Anger is not his first impulse. Compassion and mercy are.

The writer of Exodus tells a story when God wanted to destroy the people of Israel. Their leader, Moses, was on Mount Sinai for a long time, and they grew restless. They did not know where Moses was or what happened to him. Under the instruction of Moses' brother, Aaron, they made a golden calf, to which Aaron proudly introduced them, claiming this was their god to be worshiped. With that they celebrated wildly—gorging themselves on food, getting drunk and indulging in whatever felt good. They did all of this in the name of the God of Israel.

God saw this happening and became angry—so angry he wished to wipe the people of Israel off the face of the earth and start over with Moses. He told Moses his intention, and Moses did the unthinkable: he stood between God and the people of Israel.

The rabbis describe this unbelievable event by saying Moses grabbed God by the shirt and said, "Sovereign of the Universe, I will not let you go until you forgive and pardon them" (Babylonian Talmud, *Berakoth* 32a). The language and force of Moses is so strong, it's as if he pinned God to the wall, got in his face and said, "Snap out of it! This is not who you are!" God listened to Moses and decided not to go through with the punishment.

Even so, there are some who only want to speak of God's impending judgment on this world of ours. I often wonder if we should act more like Moses and beg him to show his compassion, mercy, kindness and loving faithfulness.

The tender side of God is displayed in the words of the prophet Hosea. God instructed Hosea to marry a prostitute. As expected, his wife left him, but Hosea did not give up on her. He pursued her, found her and brought her back home. All of this was a sign of Israel's relationship to her God. Even though they cheated on him, his response was to redeem them. He was a God who went to them.

Hosea went on to speak for God to the people of Israel, using the image of a mother speaking of her children. Despite God's love for them, the people continually rebelled and betrayed him. As a result his anger flared, but God did not allow his anger to lead or dictate his actions. Just as suddenly as God's anger flared up, his compassion was aroused. Again his heart turned, and his repentance was kindled. His love for his children is stronger than any anger he has toward them.

Many of us have heard stories about thundering sermons or of pastors preaching fire and brimstone. My question is, "Has it worked?" People are leaving the church in droves these days. Some think the best response is to yell louder. But maybe we need to re-think not only what we've been saying but also how we've been saying it.

If we give ourselves over to learning about God's love, we just may find that it speaks much louder than even the most brutal wrath and violence. My father experienced this when he was young. When he was in grade school, he constantly found himself in trouble. He attended a private, Catholic school and never missed an opportunity to terrorize the nuns who taught his classes. One day he went too far.

A nun grabbed him by his ear, walked him down the hallway and marched him into the principal's office. She did not want him back in her class—ever. The principal called my grandfather, and my dad waited anxiously for him to show up. Upon his arrival, my grand-father walked calmly into the principal's office and sat down. He said nothing to my father. The principal told my grandfather all the things my dad had done that day. But she did not stop there. She then detailed all of the times my dad had been in trouble.

My dad sank lower in his seat. He was ready for his father to explode at any moment, and give him a thundering smack in the back of his head. Yet as long as he waited, that never happened. He finally looked up at his father and was shocked by what he saw. Trickling down my grandfather's face was a single tear he could not hold back. He was not angry. He was filled with sorrow at all the things my dad had done.

This response was far more moving for my dad than if my grand-father had raged against him. His tenderness spoke of his deep strength. His sadness spoke of the loving heart of a father. God was in his single tear.

We must never forget that God is not anger or wrath. "God is love" (1 John 4:8). It's tempting to balk at this notion, thinking that to speak of God's love is an attempt to make faith in him more palatable. I have heard some who confidently point out that the Bible speaks far more about God's judgment and wrath than his love.

But we must remember, wrath is not who God *is*; anger is not his nature. The same cannot be said of his love. The biblical writers speak of God's love enduring forever. His wrath changes, subsides and will last only a little while. Those who insist on speaking of God's wrath, judgment and anger often underestimate the power of God's love. Love is the essence of God, while wrath is an action of God. They cannot be compared the same way. Love is who God is, was and will be. His wrath flows from his loving heart, because he cannot allow anything to ruin his good creation.

This same love compelled him to search for the man and the woman after they ate the fruit, and this same love keeps him on an endless search for all people. His love is heard in the question he asks all of us, "Where are you?" It is a love so powerful it will endure forever and ever—until all God's children are found at last. God's love runs so deep, he couldn't help but have his heart broken when he set his eyes on the miserable condition of humanity.

God instructed Noah to build a boat. And after Noah had led all the animals into the boat, his family entered as well. Then God shut the door behind them. The springs in the ground blew open and water poured down from the sky.

I often wonder what Noah and his family heard while they were locked away in the boat. What do people do when they are threatened with a flood bound to take their lives? Were people pounding on the door of the boat to get in? Did Noah and his family hear people screaming as the floodwaters grew deeper? Perhaps the most frightening part would have been the silence after the screaming and pounding stopped. Those days in the boat must have been long and difficult.

Noah and his family lived through God's destruction of everyone and everything in the known world. It rained for forty days and forty nights, and it took a year for the flood waters to recede from the earth. Noah and his family knew the day they left that boat that nothing would be the same. On the day Noah, his family and the animals emerged from the ark, they set their feet on dry ground. God went through with his plan. He took the life of every person and destroyed all living things. God rebooted creation.

After leaving the boat, Noah built an altar and performed a sacrifice to God. God was pleased with the sacrifice and said, "Never again will I curse the ground because of humans, even though every inclination of the human heart is evil from childhood" (Genesis 8:21).

Wait . . . what? Does this mean the flood didn't work?

God destroyed every living human being and the earth itself because "every inclination of the thoughts of the human heart was only evil all the time" (Genesis 6:5). Now, after calling Noah, building the ark, gathering the animals, flooding the earth and destroying humanity, he still says "every inclination of the human heart is evil." The human heart is as rotten in its core as it was before the flood. The story suggests nothing changed at all. But something did change.

After God observed every inclination of the human heart was still warped, he said, "Never again will I destroy all living creatures, as I have done" (Genesis 8:21). The human heart was unchanged but God's heart was changed. After going through with his punishment of humanity and the earth, he couldn't bear to do it again. He couldn't bear to see the suffering and the pain and the destruction.

He made a promise to never destroy the earth, animals or humans this way again. He was so sure of this that he gave himself a way of remembering his promise.

He said, "Whenever I bring clouds over the earth and the rainbow appears in the clouds, I will remember my covenant between me and you and all living creatures of every kind" (Genesis 9:14-15). Something turned in the heart of God. Before the flood, his solution was to destroy human beings because of their wickedness and violence. After, they were still violent and wicked, yet he now backed away from destroying them.

Make no mistake, God was not about to turn a blind eye toward human violence and evil. Walter Brueggemann points out that God's resolve was to let judgment and punishment fall on himself rather than to allow his wrath to fall on his creation (*Praying the Psalms,* p. 77).

What's amazing about the story of Noah is not the flood, the destruction of human life or even the destruction of the earth. It's that God made a promise to humanity, to all living creatures and to the earth itself, insisting he would never again destroy the world the way he did. God's heart broke—and that changed everything.

Building Mountains

Many in the ancient world considered mountains to be places of divine activity. Mountains rise up from the earth, the dwelling place of humanity, and ascend into the sky, the dwelling place of the gods. The ancient mind believed mountains, like temples, were the meeting place of heaven and earth, and they believed the gods lived at the top of these mountains.

I can understand why the ancients thought this way. A few miles west of where I currently sit are the awe-inspiring Rocky Mountains. Some of them tower over 14,000 feet, and the view from the top is stunning. When I have the opportunity to experience this beauty, something inside me feels deeply connected to God. At times, I too feel as though they are the intersection of heaven and earth.

But what do you do if there are no mountains? I mean, what if you live in Iowa twelve miles west of Illinois, then what? The answer is simple. You build one.

This was commonly done in the ancient Near Eastern world. They called their manmade mountains ziggurats. These towering, pyramid-like temples rose above the towns and cities. They called these temples "mountains," and they believed them to be meeting places of heaven and earth—places of divine activity.

Because these places were believed to be divine, people wrote songs and hymns to be sung in honor of them. Humans believed they had found a way to establish contact with the gods. What they had forgotten was the God who had already established contact with them. Genesis 11 tells a story about people who wanted to build a ziggurat—or mountain—reaching to the heavens. In building their mountain, they created a platform for their rule and reign on this earth. They forgot God's story, and they told a different one: a story that taught they must do something to reach God and win his favor.

We still tell this story. We live in a world that celebrates the best, biggest, wealthiest, fastest, strongest, brightest and smartest. Those at the top are the ones who receive the most accolades. If we are ever to be recognized and appreciated, then we have to do all we can too. This way of thinking is everywhere in our world.

When I started working as a pastor, I found myself constantly wanting to receive positive compliments from others. I would literally instigate conversations with others about my teaching as a roundabout way of fishing for compliments. I needed to believe I had done enough, impressed others and, in doing so, won their favor. What I came to believe was that I could build something, and not only would people love me for it but God would too.

Over time this exercise hollowed out my soul. I had built my self-worth on the idea that God and others only loved me because of what I could build. To this day, it is now easier for me to receive criticism from others than shallow praise. Empty compliments are like fuel for the fire of my belief that I have to do something to win the love, acceptance and favor of God and others.

When I was confronted with this way of thinking several years ago, I began praying the words God the Father spoke when Jesus was baptized. When Jesus came up out of the water, a voice from heaven said, "This is my Son, whom I love; with him I am well pleased" (Matthew 3:17). The beauty of these words is that God spoke them before Jesus had done anything.

Jesus had not preached, healed, walked on water, performed miracles with loaves and fishes, cast out demons, or confronted the religious leaders of his day. Jesus was the son of a God who is love, and so, he was loved. For months, I asked God to allow me to believe these words were for me too.

Then one morning, as I was getting ready to preach, I sat with my eyes closed in a gray chair in the front row of our auditorium. All around me people were standing and singing. In that moment, I was consumed by the idea of God's love for me—before I preached. God's love found me that morning, and not because of anything I did. I was struck by the notion that God does not love me because of what I can do; he loves me because of who he is. God invites us to experience his love like an ocean: wild and untamed.

Not long ago I went surfing. Let me be clear: I am not a surfer. I am a guy who can feebly stand up on a surfboard while a wave carries it along. On one such ride, something went wrong. One second I was on the board, and the next I was flying through the air, head-first, into the water.

The wave on which I was riding crashed over me and slammed me against the ocean floor. I could not believe the force of the wave. In my estimation these were small waves, but they seemed much bigger when I was being tossed around like a rag doll. I was powerless. When I finally surfaced, after what seemed like minutes, there was so much sand in my ear it felt like a starfish had been shoved in there.

Other than that I was fine due to the fact that, during the time I spent underwater, I had a moment of clarity. The first time I ever surfed, a friend told me, "If a wave grabs you, relax and go with it. You'll eventually come up. You can't fight it." He was right. The wave is a wild, powerful, untamed force no one can control. As strong as that wave was, the force of God's love is far greater.

God's love cannot be controlled or manipulated, and will always render us powerless. You cannot do anything to sway his never-ending love. The more we consider this, the more we begin to realize a God of love is to be feared far more than a God who is angry.

He is the kind of God who provides for not only those who practice justice, but also for those who are guilty of injustice. He pours out his goodness to all people, even those who are evil. God not only loves us, but he also loves the person who has caused the most pain in our life.

God's love is unfair.

Try as we might to land outside of his love, it simply can't be done. The request of love is for us to surrender to its force and discover the beauty of our powerlessness. In this we will catch glimpses of how massive God's love truly is—a beautiful and frightening thing.

His love is beautiful because God truly loves us, without the leaves on. He loves the real us. The one we find hard to look at in the mirror as we stand stark naked and feeling exposed. This is exactly why his love is so frightening. We can't imagine being seen for who we really are.

This is why I frequently pray that I would remember that I am God's son, in whom he is well pleased. I pray this because I have to; because most days, I still want to build mountains. This seems to be the condition for most people. God knows this and always has.

This is why, when he saw a mass of people building the ziggurat, he took action. He scattered those building the tower by confusing their language. All of this happened in a place called Babel. The name of this place would forever remind humanity what happens when people think they have to do things like build mountains to reach God. Even our best attempts will always fall short.

The story of the world started well but went bad quickly. Creation moved from delight to being cursed. Humanity went from being naked without shame to forming evil thoughts all the time. Add to this a flood, the destruction of humanity, a God whose heart is torn apart and humanity's continual failed attempts to reach God, and it's a tragedy of the worst kind.

Then, the story turns a corner toward hope.

For ten generations before the building of the ziggurat, God had not spoken to humanity. Now his voice shattered the silence that had persisted for generations. God spoke to a man named Abram, telling him to leave his father's house and nation and move to a new place. We know little about Abram other than his father's name and that he was seventy-five years old when God called him. Perhaps this lack of history is only right—for God's speaking to him was the day his life really began.

God promised Abram, "I will make you into a great nation, and I will bless you; I will make your name great, and you will be a blessing. I will bless those who bless you, and whoever curses you I will curse; and all peoples on earth will be blessed through you" (Genesis 12:2-3). God goes on to promise Abram and his wife, Sarai, that their descendants would be as many as the stars in the sky— like the dust of the earth. Is anyone else hearing echoes of Eden?

Eden, which was a long-forgotten memory, seemed possible again. God had a plan. He did not need humans to build mountains in an effort to reach him. He came to them. Through the promise

given to Abram, God would come to all people and bring redemption to his good creation. And he would not stop with Abram.
The promise was for his descendants and every person who would
ever live.

God told Abram his new name was Abraham, since he would be
the father of many, and his wife was to be called Sarah, as she would
be the mother of nations. Their new names would be a constant
reminder of God's promise to them. God told them he would give
them a son, and he made good on his promise.

Abraham and Sarah had a son in their old age. They named him
Isaac, and he inherited the promise God gave to his father Abraham.
Isaac had a son named Jacob, and he inherited God's promise from
Isaac. Jacob, who was later named Israel, had twelve sons. All of
them inherited the promise God had given to Abraham.

Of Jacob's twelve sons he loved one son, named Joseph, more
than the others. Jacob, not understanding subtlety very well, put
his favoritism of Joseph on display by giving Joseph an expensive
and beautiful robe. Joseph proceeded to make things worse by
telling his brothers about his dreams in which they bowed down
to him.

I was the youngest of six children, and I know that it's typically
a bad idea to do anything that resembles an attempt to upstage your
older brothers. I learned this the hard way. And just as my older
siblings often tired of listening to me, so Joseph's brothers tired
quickly of their kid brother. One day they saw their opportunity to
get rid of him.

While the brothers tended Jacob's sheep, Joseph set off to see
how they and the flock were doing in the fields. As he approached,
his brothers saw he was alone and decided to kill him. Before they
took his life, in an act of mercy the oldest son, Reuben, had a different idea. Rather than kill Joseph, they chose to sell him to the
traders for a few bucks. They covered up the sale of their brother

by putting blood on his robe and convincing their father a wild animal had eaten him. As Jacob mourned for his dead son, the traders sold Joseph into slavery in Egypt. In an incredible turn of events, Joseph went from slave to prisoner to one of the most powerful people in all of Egypt.

Long after this happened, Canaan, where Jacob and his sons lived, was struck with a severe famine. Several of Jacob's sons went to Egypt to find food, and during their time in Egypt, they came face to face once again with Joseph. The brothers did not recognize him, but he knew who they were.

Eventually Joseph told them who he was, and in a show of forgiveness, invited them and his father, Jacob, to come live in Egypt. They agreed and settled down there. This is how the book of Genesis concludes, and everything seemed to be going according to plan. That is, until the story takes one last turn.

The book of Exodus begins several generations later. Jacob and his sons' generation had died. Their descendants, the Israelites, were still in Egypt and had increased in number. Their population boom made the Egyptians nervous. They thought, if the Israelites continued to grow, they might try to take over. So they enslaved God's people.

Have you ever been in a place where things start off amazingly well? It's obvious to everyone that God is in the middle of it, and you are certain that you are exactly where God wants you—until you end up in a place of suffering. A close friend of mine experienced this exact thing when he planted a church. It was always something he believed he should do, could do and, one day, would do. Then that day came. I remember when he told me he was finally planting. The energy he and his wife had toward this was inspiring. Every detail along the way fell into place seamlessly.

People gave generously toward the church and committed to being a part of it with him. He joined with a copastor, and hundreds showed up on the first day they met. Every time we talked, he would speak with wide-eyed wonder of all that God was doing. Every day was better than the day before. Then, just a few months later, he called me to tell me he was done.

It wasn't his choice. There were a few who had joined he and his wife in helping to plant the church. He put his trust in them, but what he never knew was they did not trust him. Instead, they began to grumble and complain about his leadership, and they roped more people into their camp. They spread rumors about him, and finally, got enough leverage to tell him he had to leave.

When he called me after he was forced out, I felt terrible for him and found comforting words hard to come by. How does one reconcile this? How do you speak of a God who called him to this, provided for him and seemed to be in it every step of the way—only to let this happen? These are the kinds of questions that can come when things start off promising only to lead to unexpected pain and suffering.

This is how it was for the descendants of Abraham. They were supposed to be a sign of God's redemption for the world, but now they were brutalized, oppressed and exploited through the evil of slavery. How could this happen? How do you, as a slave in Egypt, reconcile this? What story do you tell your kids about the God of your fathers?

What would they say? Would they speak of a God who made a promise to Abraham, but somewhere along the way, he forgot? How do you explain slavery as a part of the story? We can understand these questions when we recognize that there are times when one story is about another story. So it was with the Israelites who were enslaved in Egypt.

The book of Genesis told of God creating the heavens and the earth. He placed humans, his image bearers, in his good creation, and he called them to cocreate with him. After time, they wandered far away from that call. Because of this, humanity and all creation ended up in bondage to sin and death. The earth and all humanity were slaves in need of liberation, and the journey of the people of Israel reflected this story.

Both stories began with a connection to God and great hope, but both ended in slavery. What do you do when you are suffering under the harshness of slavery? You cry out. This is what the people of Israel did. They cried out. Every day, they cried out. God heard their cry, and came to rescue them. Because God is the one who always comes to us. We don't need to build mountains to get to him.

8

You Are Me
for Everyone Else

Wake up. Work all day to the point of exhaustion in brutal conditions. Go to sleep. Wake up. Work all day to the point of exhaustion in brutal conditions. Go to sleep. Wake up. Work all day
to the point of exhaustion in brutal conditions. Go to sleep. Sound
redundant? Tiring? Imagine doing this for centuries.

This was the story of the people of Israel as slaves in Egypt. They
were brutalized every day by their Egyptian slave drivers, and every
day they cried out to God. God heard their cry and remembered his
promise to Abraham.

God delivered his people from slavery in Egypt in a miraculous
way. God bent the hard heart of Pharaoh, king of Egypt, by showing
his power through plagues sent on the Egyptians. In the end, God
proved too much for Egypt, their king and their gods. Pharaoh re-
lented, and God led his people out of Egypt.

God had liberated them, and the Israelites were now a free nation.
But the question became, "Now what?" They had been living as
slaves for four hundred years. What kind of effect does being in
slavery for this length of time have on a culture?

Your dad was a slave, and his dad was a slave. If you met a
woman at work, you knew she was a slave. If you married her

and had a daughter, she would grow up to be a slave. She might then meet a young man who was a slave, and maybe they would get married and have a child who would be a slave. This cycle went on and on for hundreds of years. Living this way would have crushed their ambitions and dreams. From the day they were born, they were told what they were going to do for the rest of their lives.

Now that God had rescued them, he came to them and told them of his intentions. He would be their king, and he invited them to be his "treasured possession." He said, "Although the whole earth is mine, you will be for me a kingdom of priests and a holy nation" (Exodus 19:5-6).

No longer would they be the workforce for Egypt; they would be a people who represented God to the world around them. No longer would Pharaoh be their king; God himself would be their king. God gave them the promises he had given to their forefather Abraham. These promises were not just for them, though; they were for everyone.

This is the promise the prophet Isaiah reflected on when he reminded the people of Israel who they were as God's nation of priests: "It is too small a thing for you to be my servant to restore the tribes of Jacob and bring back those of Israel I have kept. I will also make you a light for the Gentiles, that my salvation may reach to the ends of the earth" (Isaiah 49:6).

As a people who understood slavery and what liberation meant, they would now join God in liberating the entire world from the slavery of sin and death. As God's chosen and holy nation, they would be the ones that God would use to bring his renewal and redemption to the ends of the earth, and God himself would be with them. Anything less than this would be too small a thing for them.

As glorious as this sounds, this was a completely new reality for the people of Israel. They knew how to be slaves. They did not know how to live as a royal, holy, priestly nation. This was a new, free way of living life, one that had to be learned.

My friend Jim teaches people how to live a free life. He has given his life to serving prisoners all over the country. Nearly every day he enters jails and prisons to visit and show love to those who have been incarcerated. He has gotten to know a lot of the inmates and has heard all kinds of heartbreaking stories.

He recently met one fellow who had been released after more than thirty years in prison. He was eighteen years old when he was first incarcerated, and he was over fifty when he was released. He had never seen a laptop computer, never held a cell phone, and had heard of the Internet but did not know what it was.

After his release, life on the outside proved too much for him. He wanted to go back to prison and knew, if he were arrested again, he would spend the rest of his life behind bars. Within a few weeks of being released from prison, he robbed a store and made sure he got caught. He decided to go back to a familiar place, even if he had to lose his freedom.

Sadly, this is not an uncommon occurrence among inmates who have been locked up for a long time. They never learn what life outside of prison looks like. Often the only way they can seem to make life work, after they've been released, is to get back behind bars. Part of what Jim does is help former inmates learn about a life of freedom so they do not have to go back.

Long before inmates are ever released, he connects them to mentors who teach them about life on the outside. Those mentors are with them the day they are released and they walk with them for years after. When this happens, less than 5 percent of inmates return to prison. The difference? They learn how to live in freedom.

This kind of living has to be learned, which is why, when God invited Israel to be his people, he began by teaching them what a free life looks like.

His first words to them were, "I am the LORD your God, who brought you out of Egypt, out of the land of slavery" (Exodus 20:2). Slavery was no doubt a fresh memory for the people of Israel, as was their miraculous rescue from it, but God still saw it necessary to remind them that Egypt was a land of slavery.

In the ancient world, Egypt was not typically thought of in terms of slavery. Egypt was the wealthiest, most powerful empire of its day. It was home to the Nile River, which ensured bountiful crops. It was a sophisticated and wealthy land with a strong military. To speak of Egypt, then, was to speak of wealth and power.

Yet for those who had just been delivered from slavery, to mention Egypt was to speak of an empire of oppression. Why did God have to remind them of this? It had only been three months; had they forgotten how terrible Egypt was? Apparently they had.

Not long after God rescued them from Egypt, they complained against Moses and longed to go back to Egypt. They said, "There we sat around pots of meat and ate all the food we wanted" (Exodus 16:3). In that moment of desperation, they forget about the forced labor, the oppression and the brutality. In that moment in their memories, Egypt became a place of provision.

Humanity has not changed all that much over thousands of years. How often, when the pressure is put on us, do we want to go back to what we know? I have a friend who is a recovering alcoholic. He has told me, when life gets tough, often the first thing that comes to his mind is, "I should go get drunk." Even though alcohol cost him his family, his job, his money and almost his life, he is still tempted to go back.

We will instinctively run to what we know, even if it is self-destructive—because, at least, we know it. It feels safe, there is a sense of security, we even believe that we can control it, and we tell ourselves, "It will be different this time." Slavery can look good when we are desperate.

Unless Egypt was remembered as slavery, in a moment of desperation, the people may have wanted to go back. They may have begun to live as slaves again, even treating one another as slaves. This could not happen. They were not slaves anymore. They were liberated people who were a holy nation. If Egypt was not remembered rightly, they may just repeat it.

God was opening up a new way of life, the kind of life free people live. If they are free people, they will bring liberation to others—because true freedom never enslaves or oppresses others. The good news is that Israel would not have to figure out how to do this alone; God would be with them every step of the way. When he led the people out of Egypt, he appeared to them like a pillar of cloud during the day and at night like a pillar of fire. They knew God was with them in that desert, that he was always in their midst. God even instructed them to build him a tent for him to live in, because sometimes *we* need something concrete and real.

While ideas are good and words can be comforting, being able to touch, see and feel is often far better. The people heard the voice of God, and they witnessed his miracles, but now God's tent was right next to theirs. Isn't this how God works? If the people of Israel had to live in tents in the middle of the desert, then God would live in a tent in the desert too. It's as though God was saying, "I'm with you in this one."

They called the tent God lived in the tabernacle, and when they finished building it, God's glory filled the tent. The Israelites did not have to build anything to get themselves *up* to God. Rather, he asked the Israelites to build something among them as a constant reminder that he was with them, right where they were, while they lived in the desert.

They lived in tents in the desert for forty years, and then God led them into the land he promised to Abraham. This land was a good and fertile land that yielded large amounts of food. The land produced so much food that no one ever had to go hungry. No one had to be so poor they could not feed themselves. God made good on his promise to bless Abraham and his descendants.

The story of Israel is about God being *with* his people and leading them into a new land that would provide food, contentedness, freedom and everyone having enough. This land would give them everything they would ever need or want. When the biblical writers described the land that God had promised to Abraham, they spoke of a place that was more than the good life; it sounded like Eden.

Yet this was not only for their benefit but for the benefit of all people. They were to be an enduring picture of what life looks like when God is your king. As a royal, holy nation of priests, they would participate with God in his renewal and redemption of the entire world.

Many generations after Israel settled in the land, Solomon built a temple for God in the city of Jerusalem. He dedicated the temple, asking God to hear the prayers of anyone who came to that temple so that "all the peoples of the earth may know your name and fear you" (1 Kings 8:43). This temple was not only for the people of Israel but for all people on earth. God's glory filled the temple. God came and dwelled with them. This temple was to be a sign to the world that God lived among his people; it was the place where heaven and earth met.

Humanity was once again connected to God, and God was with them. It was like Eden all over again. Everything seemed to be looking up. They had the chance to participate with God in being a light for all people. But like the other stories that ended in slavery, this one did too.

What started with so much promise and hope eventually spiraled downward. King Solomon forced slaves to be his workforce in Israel. He had nearly 1,000 wives, and they taught him to worship other gods. In the generations after Solomon, many kings and the people of Israel did evil in the eyes of God.

They were liberated slaves but now they enslaved others. God lived with them, yet they worshiped other gods and built other temples in hopes of connecting with them. They oppressed the poor and cared little for God's good gifts to them. They forgot God's commandments, teaching them how to live free lives, and they exchanged liberation for enslavement. Like all who ever lived before them, they believed they could find love apart from God.

Their actions led to God's judgment: The Babylonians waged war against them and Jerusalem was destroyed. The temple was torn down and burned, and the people of Israel were exiled to Babylon— the same place where people were trying to build mountains to reach the gods.

This only serves to remind us that trying to find love apart from God will always lead to the same place, over and over again.

This is not far from the definition of insanity: repeatedly doing the same thing and expecting different results. Sin is no different. As much as we keep doing it, we rarely seem to realize it produces the same thing—namely anxiety, sorrow, grief and, eventually, death. When the people of Israel forgot about being liberated from slavery, they enslaved others. And when they enslaved others, it led to their own enslavement once again.   *Amen* .

This is how it works: Anytime we search for life, freedom, love or hope apart from God, we will only end up more lost—or, in the case of Israel, enslaved. This is what the stories found in the Hebrew Scriptures teach us. They tell one story about three different groups of people: the stories of the first man and first woman, the sons of Jacob in Egypt and the nation of Israel all end in slavery. The first two tell of God liberating the people from slavery but not the third. Yet in the midst of this heartache, the prophets spoke of a faint glimmer of hope.

They told of a time when God would return to his people and rescue them. They even spoke about the temple being rebuilt. Jeremiah, speaking for God, wrote of a day that would come when the people would return from the land of their enemies, come to the temple and "shout for joy" (Jeremiah 31:12-16). The prophets spoke comfort to the people of Israel, telling them God would do a new work.

The people were even described as a "well-watered garden" (Jeremiah 31:12). A garden? The prophets could not conceive of anything better than a garden. Of course, not just any garden, they spoke of Eden itself. The prophet Isaiah told the people of Israel that God would make their "deserts like Eden" (Isaiah 51:3). The prophet Ezekiel wrote that God would rebuild ruins and said the wasteland would "become like the garden of Eden" (Ezekiel 36:35). The prophet Joel spoke to the richness of the land that God would renew, and he compared the splendor to the Garden of Eden (Joel 2:3). The prophets gave the people hope, but sometimes hope is hard to come by.

Seventy years after the people of Israel were exiled, some were allowed to return to Jerusalem to rebuild the city and the temple. As exciting as this seemed, they soon realized nothing was the same. The temple wasn't as glorious as the one Solomon built. Even worse, when the new temple was built and dedicated, the glory of God did not fill the temple as it did the tabernacle and the first temple. Amidst all the hope, the promises, the anticipation, the talk of Eden, it seemed God was nowhere. After a few years of this, one might have begun to wonder if he would ever show up.

What would have been going through your mind during this time? Imagine growing up and hearing legendary stories about God rescuing Israel from Egypt, stories about the kings of Israel, stories about the splendor of Solomon's temple and what it was like the day the glory of God filled it. People might have talked a lot about the "good old days" when things were better.

Many of us know exactly how this feels. We hear people speak about God, his presence, his love, his grace or how he has answered prayers. Like the people waiting for God's glory to show up in the temple, we wonder if any of this is really true. It would be one thing if we cried out to God and he answered, but what about when he is silent?

What happens when it seems that God does not say a word? There was a time in my life when I experienced this kind of silence from God. I began to wonder if there even was a God. During that time, I was lonely, scared and wounded. One night I was in my car on a crystal clear, winter night. Even though I was in the city, I could see the stars brightly shining. I pulled up to a stoplight, and looked out my window at the stars. God seemed to be somewhere beyond them, too busy to pay attention to me. Overwhelmed by that feeling and filled with rage, I screamed out, "What is wrong with you? You are screwing me! Do you even care one bit about what I am going through?"

Silence. *I know this*

Have you ever asked questions like this? "God, are you out there?" or "Where were you when I was hurting?" Maybe, like the psalmists, you've shaken your fist at God and asked if he was deaf. If you have felt the pain of longing, if you have experienced the elusiveness of hope, if you have ever cried out in total, exasperated despair—wishing you could catch just a glimpse of evidence that might show God is possibly around—you are not alone.

This is where the people of Israel were—enslaved, waiting, longing and crying out for God to return. This is how the third story ends. While Eden was their hope, for the time being it was a distant memory. Nothing seemed to go right. The people cried out every day, "How long, O Lord?" And we are left to wonder if God had finally given up—or if he would once again do all he could to reach out to humanity.

9

Take Me Back to the Start

Sometimes there are certain words or particular phrases that capture our attention. The actual words themselves may not mean much, but the context or place in which we hear them can fill us with meaning and bring about strong reactions. This can be understood if we pause to consider three things: oceans, mountains and sharks.

The two places I love more than anywhere on this earth are the ocean and the mountains—specifically the beaches of Southern California and the Rocky Mountains of Colorado. Both are indescribably beautiful, powerful and beyond taming, but in very different ways and for very different reasons. The massive difference between the two places can be understood when we think of how certain words would be heard in both places: a word used in one place will capture attention, while doing little or nothing in the other place.

Every summer my family and I spend time in Southern California. We spend many days on the beach, building sand castles, throwing the Frisbee, playing in the water, bodyboarding and surfing. Of course, there are inherent dangers in the ocean, which bring us to sharks.

If I were to stand on the beach and frantically scream, "Shark!" I suspect anyone who heard me would be struck with fear and would

get out of the water as quickly as possible. Everyone who has seen
Shark Week knows the sharks always win. But there are times when
screaming the word *shark* would do little to trouble anyone. This
brings us to mountains.

One of my favorite mountain towns in Colorado is Telluride. Its
beauty is unmatched. If I was there and walked around the town
screaming "Shark!" all anyone would think is that I had lost my
mind or had spent too much time at a local drinking establishment.
There would be little concern for anyone's safety.

The ocean and the mountains give meaning to someone screaming
about sharks, because sometimes the context determines how one
hears and understands certain words. Then John, a disciple of Jesus,
wrote a Gospel. He began with these words, "In the beginning." It
was far more than a clever way of referring back to creation. If we
pause to consider the context of the people of Israel, then we will
understand why those words would grab their attention.

Seventy years after Israel was exiled to Babylon, they were allowed
to return to Jerusalem to rebuild the city walls and the temple, and
they did just that. Once again, they were free to worship in the
temple and live in Jerusalem. Even still, many believed they were
still slaves. For nearly four hundred years before John wrote his
Gospel, foreign empires occupied the land and oppressed the
people of Israel.

In those days, hope seemed like a foolish thing. Believing the
promises of God, while oppression and persecution were a daily
reality, seemed impossible. The Israelites lived each day wondering
where God was while they were under the rule of godless empires
and violent kings like Antiochus Epiphanes.

His empire ruthlessly oppressed the people for years. In one fit of rage against the people of Israel, he went to Jerusalem bent on destroying everyone and everything. In just three days, more than 40,000 people were massacred. Blood flowed in the streets as young and old people were butchered—even children and infants were savagely slaughtered. The 40,000 who survived were sold into slavery.

Antiochus then made laws against the Jewish people, and if they were found practicing their faith, they would be killed. He destroyed any copy of the Hebrew Scriptures he could find, and he transformed God's temple into one to the god Jupiter.

The Jewish temple was the most sacred place on earth for the people of Israel, and now worshipers of Jupiter went to God's temple to engage in ritual sex acts with temple prostitutes. On the altar where the people of Israel offered sacrifices as a pleasing aroma to God, pigs, the most unclean animal for the Jewish people, were sacrificed.

Surely, God would return and judge Antiochus. According to the psalmist, only those who had clean hands, a pure heart and did not trust in false gods could ascend God's holy hill where his temple was. Now Antiochus and his people ascended his holy hill and desecrated the temple. Would God stand for this? Perhaps after hundreds of years of silence, God would finally return. Maybe Eden was just around the corner. This hope hung in the heart of every person in Israel.

Yet, day after day, God was silent. As you can imagine, some could not stand by and watch Antiochus and his people do such things. After years of living in an occupied land, there was a revolt in Israel. Within a few years, the Jewish people regained control of Jerusalem and purified and rededicated the temple. There was a time of great celebration that the Jewish people remember to this day when they celebrate Hanukkah. But even in that celebration and in the dedication of the temple, God did not fill it with his glory

like he did in the days of Solomon. The question remained: When
would God return for his people?

Not long after they won their freedom from Antiochus, Jerusalem was sacked again. Eventually the Roman Empire rose to
power and conquered Jerusalem under the leadership of a Roman
military general by the name of Pompey. The Romans allowed
temple worship to continue, but they appointed the high priest and
the governor of Judea to ensure control of religion and politics.

Towering over the temple courts was the Antonia Fortress. It was
a military stronghold for the Romans in the city and a constant
reminder to the Jewish people of their oppressor. It was built high
enough for the Roman military to view the temple so they could
keep an eye on the Jewish people, making sure they would not attempt another revolt.

The Jewish people lived under the occupation of a foreign military superpower. They waited and longed for God to show up and
deliver them. All the senseless deaths, pain, suffering, oppression,
cries, longing and anticipation reached a fever pitch in the years
Rome occupied the land of Israel. Oppression was their context.

Then, one night, in the small town of Bethlehem on the outskirts
of Jerusalem, a child was born to a virgin who was pledged to be
married to a man named Joseph. They named this child Jesus,
which brings us back to the words John wrote in his Gospel, "In
the beginning."

The words "in the beginning" told the story of the time when
God created the heavens and the earth as his temple—a time when
the man and the woman had perfect harmony with God and one
another. If you lived when John was writing, what meaning would
your context give to those words?

For the people of Israel, Eden was not just a story from long ago.
Eden was their hope for the future. It spoke of the way the world
once was and the way the world would one day be again. Every cry

ringing out from the people of Israel reflected a longing to return to the start, to go back to the beginning. John's Gospel told the people this was possible.

By returning to the opening words of the Bible, he insisted Jesus' story did not begin in a stable. He wrote that Jesus was with God in the beginning, because Jesus is, in fact, God. He explained all things were made by him and through him, and he is the one who brought life and light to all things (John 1:1-4). This is the God Israel longed for. He had returned to his people—just not the way they expected.

He did not come to the temple and fill it with his glory. No, he was the temple. John wrote that God himself put on flesh and lived among us. Another way of saying this is to say Jesus was the tabernacle. Just as God came to his people Israel, rescued them from slavery in Egypt and lived among them in a tent, now God in Jesus came to the people of Israel to rescue them and live among them in flesh and bone.

God was saying to his people, "If you have to live, suffer and die here on this earth then so will I." In Jesus, we hear God saying to humanity, "I'm with you on this one." When you are telling a story this big, you have to start at the beginning. If you don't, nothing will make any sense. That's how it is with some stories.

When I was in college, I went home for a weekend and found my sister watching a film about some people in prison. I sat down and asked about certain characters and why they were in prison. Each time I asked, she just told me to be quiet. I finally asked her what film it was, and she said it was called *The Shawshank Redemption*.

Within a few minutes of watching the film, I figured out something had gone wrong in the prison. Someone named Andy Dufresne was missing, and no one knew where he was. Several people were in his cell, one of whom was the prison warden and he was especially angry. In his frustration he threw a rock at a poster of Raquel Welch, which hung on a wall in the cell. When the stone went through the paper, there was the sound of a rock bouncing across concrete.

Everyone in the cell was puzzled. The warden ripped the poster off the wall and found a tunnel that it took Andy more than two decades to dig out. The tunnel went through the wall of the prison and eventually led to his freedom. The next several scenes in the film showed Andy's carefully planned escape, and culminated with Andy standing outside the prison. He raised his arms toward the sky as rain poured down on him. He was free.

It was obvious something big had happened here, but I had no idea what it was. As my sister was fighting back tears, I was confused and asked, "Wait, who is Andy Dufresne?" Over the next few weeks my sense of missing out only grew. It seemed everyone spoke of how much they loved the film, which only made me want to see the movie more.

Eventually I did, and I watched it from the beginning. I learned of Andy Dufresne, knew his story and understood his place in the film. Even though I had seen the warden throw the rock through the poster of Raquel Welch, the scene was more amazing the second time. And when Andy stood outside the prison with his hands raised, I raised my hands up in the air with him. The whole story made sense because I had started at the beginning.

Have you ever felt like you've missed something when it comes to the story of Jesus? His story is good and certainly amazing, but at times it feels like we are walking in on the last ten minutes of a film. Perhaps, this is why we are tempted to think God was pacing the floor of heaven, nervously biting his fingernails, and wondering if this business of redemption and renewal was ever going to work.

We can think that Jesus' reason for coming here was because God wanted to do things himself, since no one else could get it right. We might think of the story of Jesus in all sorts of ways, struggling to fully understand what is happening—especially if we fail to start at the beginning.

John wants us to see that the story of Jesus only makes sense if we understand the story of the Bible. When John starts his Gospel with the words, "In the beginning," we are reminded of the first man and the first woman who lived in perfect harmony in the Garden of Eden. We remember their choice and how the sin of humanity grew until God saw every thought of humanity was only evil all the time. As humanity chose to carve out its path of death and destruction, God called Abraham and promised he would bless him *and* all people who would ever live.

God remembered this promise to Abraham when the people of Israel were in slavery in Egypt and he rescued them. He delivered them from slavery and called them to live as a royal, holy, priestly nation. They were to play a central role in the redemption of the world. The promise given to Abraham and the call placed on Israel were fulfilled in the person of Jesus.

Jesus is the apex of Israel's story. This is why Matthew began his Gospel with a genealogy. He showed Jesus to be a descendant of Abraham. As a descendant, Jesus was the fulfillment of God's promise that all people who ever lived would be blessed through Abraham and his descendants. Through Jesus, Israel claimed her rightful place at the center of God's story of redeeming the world.

But this redemption came at a price. So far, this sounds like a wonderful story about promises and blessing, but there is the dark side. Part of the story is about the sin and brokenness of humanity, and God had seen this part and his heart broke—and that changed everything. When we go back to the beginning, we understand that, in Jesus, we encounter God, who has chosen to take on the suffering and punishment that had fallen on his creation.

Jesus, through his life, death, burial and resurrection made good on the promises God gave to Abraham, his descendants and the world. In a way no one expected, Jesus brought the longed-for freedom, restoration, liberation, renewal and redemption. You can't start a story like this anywhere else but the beginning. God had come, put on flesh and bone, and lived among us.

When the people of Israel read how John started his Gospel, they knew that God had not given up on them, on humanity and on his good creation. The person of Jesus showed the world, in a way no one else could, that God is the one who is doing all he can to get to us.

10

That's It, but Not All

Sometimes when I hear people speak about Jesus' coming to earth, his death, burial and resurrection, it sounds completely underwhelming. Can I be honest about that? I do not think his death is something to be ignored or that it's no big deal. But at times, it seems rather small and inconsequential in the cosmic sense.

Let me explain.

Several years ago, just after the Christmas and New Year's holiday season, I met with a fellow from our church. We met at one of my favorite places in town, The Pub on Pearl, and we sat down at a high-top table near the front door.

We made small talk for a time, asking all the normal post-holiday questions: "How was your Christmas?" "Did you travel or stay in town?" "What did you do for the New Year?" After these questions were asked and answered, he jumped right into the reason he wanted to meet.

He said, "I think I need to leave the church." I was caught off guard. He then quickly clarified, "Well, not *the* church, but *this* church." I went from feeling caught off guard to feeling stung. I know several pastors who say they are not concerned about who decides to become a part of their congregation and others who claim they are not concerned about those who leave. Truth be told,

I am more concerned about followers of Jesus finding their place in the kingdom. But this was different. This was a friend.

This was someone who I knew before I became a pastor at Denver Community Church. He was deeply invested in several people in the congregation. To hear him say, "*this* church," with such emphasis, stung. I tried, unconvincingly, to hide my wincing face. He stared into his beer as he told me his reasons for wanting to leave. None of the reasons really seemed true. Even the way he spoke made me think he wasn't telling the whole story. He paused for a moment, and I asked, "Is there anything else?"

He looked me in the eye and said, "You don't preach the gospel." The words came tumbling out of his mouth awkwardly, like Lego blocks tumbling out of a bag onto a concrete floor, making a lot of noise and bouncing everywhere. He stopped and realized he wanted to say more. "Not once, in all your sermons, have I heard the gospel. If I did not know Jesus and I came to this church, I would have no idea how to accept him as my Savior and go to heaven. Sometimes it seems like you are going to talk about the gospel but you don't, and I can't be a part of a church where the gospel is not preached."

His words seemed to echo for a moment around the pub. I admired his honesty. In that moment I completely agreed and disagreed with him. His understanding of the gospel taught that the death of Jesus is how God chose to take care of individual sin, making a way for us to go to heaven when we die. My sin has brought separation from God, and because God is holy, he cannot be around sin.

Furthermore, because God is just, he demands punishment for my sin. The punishment I deserve is death; that is my debt. No matter how hard I try, I will never be able to pay off the debt. The good news is God, in his graciousness, did not abandon us in our time of need. He sent his Son, Jesus, to us, and he died the death none of us could die. The death of Jesus paid off my debt. If I believe in this and accept Jesus as my Savior, then I am assured of going to heaven.

I've heard this gospel from many. It's not that this message is wrong; it's just incomplete. It's only a part of the larger story.

Yet, for my friend, this is what he understood the gospel to be. He was right to say we had never preached the gospel at one of our Sunday gatherings—at least not the way he thought of it. At the same time, at our weekly Sunday gatherings, we *do* preach the gospel. Our sermons explore the length, breadth, depth and height of the good news of the kingdom of heaven. In all we do, we are constantly opening ourselves to the cosmic scope of the gospel, and waking up a little more each day to the fact that it is good news for all people.

As we neared the end of our time together, my friend leaned forward on his elbows, folded his hands under his chin and said, "I really love you and what you are doing. I will continue to pray for you guys." I knew he was serious. More so, I loved and still do love his good heart and his passion for Jesus.

When we left, he walked to his car and I walked back to our church building. The sun was beginning its early evening descent, and my mind went over our conversation. How had two friends— who were a part of the same faith community, who had similar ideas about God—come to such different conclusions about the gospel? Conclusions that, in the mind of my friend, were serious enough for him to leave the church?

Was our understanding of the gospel vastly different, or were we just talking in different ways about the same thing? Was one of us completely wrong, or were we both a little right? Is it possible that the gospel is bigger than a personal conversion experience? All of this got me thinking long and hard about the massive story we call "the gospel." Too often, in an effort to understand it, we end up limiting the gospel.

Whenever the gospel is a simple matter of any one person getting his or her sin taken care of and getting their ticket punched to heaven, it is a reduction of a larger story. With this kind of thinking, the gospel can move from being centered on the person of Jesus, and it can become centered on you and me. The story becomes about our sin, our salvation and our ability to live forever in heaven.

It can serve as a form of escapism. Heaven becomes the goal and the reward for us. If we stop there, the gospel is just a story about something God has done for our benefit. *This is not the gospel.* This message is an invitation to experience personal salvation, but contrary to the belief of some, this is not the central issue of the gospel.

The gospel is a story not only about something done for us but also about something God wants to do in us and through us. As the people of God, we cannot forget that we exist for the benefit of all people. Anytime the gospel becomes a story about privilege alone, we have missed the mark. This is why there are times when I hear people speak about the death of Jesus, and it feels underwhelming.

But more than merely being underwhelming, limiting the gospel story this way can lead to confusion and raise all kinds of questions. In my experience, this limiting story leaves many uncertain about God, the nature of forgiveness, the reality of sin and why Jesus had to die in the first place. Questions are asked, and they seem to have no good answer.

Questions like: Did Jesus really *need* to die so God could forgive our sins? Doesn't this suggest God was somehow restricted by sin? Was he limited to only one choice? Did he find it more reasonable to punish sins rather than forgive them? Did we really owe God a debt we couldn't pay, or was the debt owed to someone or something else? In paying the debt, did God really have to punish another member of the Trinity with such violence? If he did, then what kind of God is he? Is he safe? Can we trust him? Is it safe to say Jesus was really saving us from God? Is God, ultimately, a vindictive, vengeful God who is seeking retribution? Did Jesus save us from God's retribution? Did Jesus, in his death, earn God's forgiveness on our behalf? And why, before Jesus died, did he tell people their sins were forgiven? And if God the Father is the only one who can forgive sins, then why did Jesus say he had authority to forgive sins? Is this the gospel, the good news about the kingdom of heaven, that Jesus preached? Is this what the story of the cross is all about: getting our sin removed so we can access God?

Questions like these come about, in part, because we have left out a massive and central part of the gospel. When this happens, we are guilty of making the gospel too small, and it no longer bears mystery or wonder. I don't know about you, but I don't want to limit the good news of Jesus. I want a story far bigger than me, a story like the one the biblical writers told and the early church proclaimed.

They claimed the gospel was not about Jesus *only* coming to pay a debt. The good news was so much more! The good news was about the redemption, and restoration, of all things in heaven and on earth. The gospel told the story of how Jesus' life, death, burial and resurrection forever defeated the powers of sin and death. As a result, the entire creation will one day be liberated, and we are able to live freely and forgiven as we join with God in his renewal of all creation.

Amen

Paul, in his letter to the church in Rome, said sin entered the world through one man. Sin ravaged the earth, actively working against God's good creation, and sin brought death to all humanity. Now through Jesus, the earth will be repaired and God's creation will again become good, and through Jesus' resurrection, all people can be made alive.

The gospel is the story of how God is reclaiming what has been his all along. We cannot forget that, when God created the heavens and the earth, he saw all he had created and called it "good." This was not a casual feeling God had. His words meant creation was soaked with God's goodness. In other words, it was perfect.

Sometimes it's easy to forget how good God's creation is. When I first moved to Denver, I nearly got into a car accident every day. I could not keep my eyes on the road because I kept staring at the mountains. One morning the beauty of the mountains especially captivated me. It had snowed the night before, and the mountains were stunning—brilliant white against the backdrop of the deep blue sky. I asked my friend Jon if he saw the mountains on the way into work that morning.

Jon grew up and had been surrounded by this unbelievable beauty his entire life. He said, "No. Honestly, I don't look at the mountains anymore." Nothing in me understood how a person could ever stop basking in the beautiful views we have in Denver. However, years later, I was guilty of the same thing: I stopped looking at the mountains too. While this made me a better driver, I forgot how good God's creation was.

Then something happened this summer. My son and I went backpacking. We hiked up toward three mountains, nicknamed the "Three Apostles." They rise sharply out of the earth, and have rugged peaks of more than 13,000 feet. Sprawling at the foot of these peaks is a mountain meadow with a small creek running through it. It is filled with lush, green grass and millions of wildflowers. We hiked into the meadow, took a break and sat on a large rock to have a snack.

As we ate, I noticed my son was silent. I looked at him and saw he was staring at the Three Apostles. He was fixated. For nearly twenty minutes we sat in complete silence, soaking in the indescribable beauty all around us. It had been a long time since I had sat quietly and basked in God's good creation. In the times I do, I am reminded why God called it *good*.

This is what the psalmist reflected when he considered God's handiwork. He wrote, "The heavens declare the glory of God; the skies proclaim the work of his hands. Day after day they pour forth speech; night after night they reveal knowledge" (Psalm 19:1-2). This handiwork of God is what the powers of darkness ravaged.

God was not about to look at what had happened to his good creation and say, "Well it was good while it lasted. What next?" Not a chance. That would be quitting and giving the win to the evil one. God could not stand by and watch his good creation be destroyed any longer. His plan was to redeem what was rightfully his.

This is what Paul meant when he said, through Jesus, God was reconciling all things to himself. God is interested in seeing all things redeemed—not just you and me. Paul wanted to be sure we did not miss what he meant when he said "all things." So he added "whether things on earth or things in heaven" (Colossians 1:15-20). In case you missed his point, he means *everything* in *all* of creation: rocks, moons, relationships, squirrels, our work, streams, stellar nebula, trees, our desires—all things will be reconciled. *Amen* !

To reconcile is to bring something back into a harmony that once existed, and God is not the one who is out of tune. All things are being reconciled to him; he is not the one who has to reconcile himself to all things. And all things are being reconciled to him through the death of Jesus on the cross. Through this he will bring peace, wholeness and healing.

This is the hope for all creation. Though God's good world has been frustrated and groans in the pains of childbirth, through Jesus all creation "will be liberated from its bondage to decay and brought into the freedom and glory of the children of God" (Romans 8:21). In this, God will bring "unity to all things in heaven and on earth under Christ" (Ephesians 1:10).

No doubt, this is a cosmic story. Do you see how, when we think the entirety of the gospel is just about our sin and getting to heaven, it can feel underwhelming? We ought never think we have come to the place where we can package the gospel and be done with it. Rather, we must always find ways to keep talking about it. News this good must be told and retold, because some things are beyond words. Certain times defy explanation.

After the birth of my children, I could not fully describe the absolute and total joy I experienced. My heart broke with happiness. How do you tell someone about that? If all I had said was, "my wife gave birth to a child," well, yes, that would have been true, but that explanation would have felt incomplete.

I will never forget the day I was married. When I saw my wife at the end of the aisle, hanging on to her dad's arm, tears filled my eyes and my breath was gone. The moment was sacred and holy. To this day I cannot express how my heart stirred when I saw her. What would it be like if all I said was, "Yep, she was wearing a nice dress and looked pretty"? True, it was a nice dress, and she looked beautiful, but is that all I can say? That's only part of the story.

If we can talk forever about memorable, beautiful moments, which are locked into our memory, with our friends and family, then how much more the gospel? Are we content with thinking of it as a presentation? Is it enough to make the good news of Jesus only about our sin and getting our ticket punched for heaven?

The gospel of Jesus Christ is a story far bigger than we can imagine. As such, we should never tire of telling and retelling. As the people of God, we should have deep joy as we continually discover new contours to this cosmic redemption story. In this, we will learn it is not just a story to be told but one that invites us to participate in it. And not only participate but play a central role, because the start of God's redemption begins with us, his image bearers.

When sin entered the world, it started with a person. The result was sin spilled out into God's good creation. In the person of Jesus, the renewal, redemption and restoration God had promised entered the world. His redemption began with *individuals* and moved out into the world. This is important for us to grasp, because with a story this colossal, it can be hard to see where we fit.

At times it's easy to feel lost amidst God's story. For much of my life I felt this way. Occasionally I was so uncertain about my place, I supposed I would be the one who was left out. My heart really did want to see the hope and healing of Jesus poured out on this world. The problem was, I was not sure the same hope and healing would be given to me. I held on to so many moments of shame, hurt and pain. I chose to believe the lies about who I was that were hidden deep inside. This way of thinking was pervasive in my mind. I once told a friend I felt my lot in life was to help as many people as possible off a sinking boat into a life raft—all the while knowing that I would never make it in the life raft myself.

Then one day all that changed. God spoke to me in a way that forever reshaped my heart. I know when some hear the words "God spoke to me," there are questions about what that means. I like to say that our souls have ears, and those ears are perfectly designed to hear the voice of God if we agree to listen. So it was on this day.

I was alone in a small chapel. As hard as it was, I chose to sit in silence and asked God to speak to me. He did. He said, "Michael, do you see all the renewal, redemption and restoration I am doing in this world? I want to do it in you too." And I was undone.

I wept for days because, for the first time, I saw the massive, cosmic story of the gospel—which has the power to redeem all of creation—was also at work in my bruised, battered and broken heart. This is why the gospel is so beautiful. It is universal in its scope yet extremely personal and intimate in its healing of you and me. This is why we will forever be able to speak of the good news, discovering new words and ways of expressing the vast truth of God's story.

That day was a restart in my journey as a beloved son of the Almighty God. Most of my life I spent feeling completely lost because *I* kept trying to find my way out—and that only made things worse. On that day, I realized that all my searching was not to find God but to be found by him. This was a miracle because, for so long, I never believed I was worth finding. God found me, and I had no idea how far he was willing to go for that to happen.

A Theology of Graffiti

Rome was built on seven hills. The hill in the center was the Palatine Hill. On the northwestern side of this hill, Emperor Tiberius lived in a sprawling palace. After his death, his palace became a boarding school for training young men for imperial service. In the ruins of this school, graffiti was discovered.

The graffiti wasn't much different than what we might see today. Graffiti is on nearly every wall, garage door and billboard in the neighborhood where I live. What the aspiring, vandalistic artists who decorate my neighborhood do not know is that they are part of a centuries-old tradition. People have been creating unauthorized artwork for more than 2,000 years.

The graffiti discovered on the Palatine Hill in Rome speaks toward how Romans viewed early Christians. It also speaks toward how they viewed Jesus himself. Many believed worshiping Jesus was the height of stupidity.

One Roman thinker, Marcus Cornelius Fronto, claimed the entire Christian religion was foolish. He said this because he saw Christians worshiping a crucified man who had the "head of an ass" (Minucius Felix, *The Octavius,* chap. IX). Fronto was not alone. Archaeologists discovered graffiti in Rome that suggested others thought the same thing of Jesus. The image shown below is what they found:

Figure 11.1.

Beside the cross is a young man, hand raised in homage, worshiping this donkey-headed figure. Beneath the drawing are the
words: *Alexamanos cebete theon*, translated as "Alexamanos worships [his] god." While some find this offensive, perhaps we should
embrace this work of art as good theology.

After all, Paul was quick to point out that the "message of the
cross is foolishness" (1 Corinthians 1:18). He claimed that, through
this foolishness, Jesus "disarmed the powers and authorities, he
made a public spectacle of them, triumphing over them by the
cross" (Colossians 2:15).

Most anyone in Paul's day would have thought he was out of his
mind to think a victim of crucifixion had "triumphed." Obviously,
they did not triumph; they died. And therein lies the upside-down
nature of true strength in the kingdom of heaven: what's strong is
weak, and what's weak is strong.

Jesus broke the power of sin and death, showing us that, within
the kingdom of God, life and not death has the final word. Jesus

won by losing, and through his loss, we have life. He did not play by the rules of the empires. He stared down and defeated their greatest weapon—death itself. He showed, once and for all, the power of God's kingdom.

People in Rome would have laughed at such nonsense. And this is exactly what Fronto and this graffiti artist did. They thought Jesus was an ass. Perhaps this perspective was due not only to the way he died but also to the way he lived his life.

The Gospel writers were careful to point out the kind of person Jesus was. He lived a scandalous life. He hung out with sluts, corrupt businessmen and those whom the religious called "sinners." Not only did he hang out with them, but he also ate meals with them. This was unthinkable in Jesus' day. If these people were known as sinners for what they did in public, then just imagine what they did behind closed doors. So, they assumed, when Jesus was behind those closed doors with these people, then he must be doing all the things they did. And if he wasn't, well then he was guilty by association.

His guilt came because of what meals expressed in his day. If someone in Jesus' day invited you to dinner, it was a major event. Meals were far more than enjoying some food and wine; they expressed friendship, unity and intimacy. For some, meals were one way of distancing themselves from the unholy people in Israel. Meals acted as a way to divide the classes—religiously, socially and economically. But not for Jesus. He had no problem eating meals in the homes of sinners and tax collectors.

In fact, Jesus' habit of eating and drinking with these sinners led some to accuse him of being a glutton, a drunkard and a friend of tax collectors. Tax collectors were known for their dishonesty and the exploitation of their own people. Many in the Jewish world shunned these people because they worked for Rome. Not Jesus; he was their friend. He was not willing to withdraw from a world that many who were pious considered sinful. We can learn something from this. Too often, those who follow Jesus are only interested in withdrawing from this world and our culture.

Maybe this attitude is precisely the reason our world is so broken. Perhaps our world is so dark because so few choose to go to the dark places with the light of Jesus and his hope that brings healing. Rather than take the risk of going there, we build walls instead of pathways. We hole up in a world of our own creation.

A few weeks ago, I spoke with someone I dearly love. She told me about a party she attended and how awful the whole thing was, and how many people there made her uncomfortable. The moment she entered the home, she knew she was definitely not like them. Most importantly, she explained how they knew she was not like them.

This made me wonder if the sinners who ate food and drank wine with Jesus felt like he was not one of them. Did they get the sense he looked around and compared himself to them?

⊕

If we are to be like Jesus, we must be willing not only to help out those who are marginalized in our world, but also to associate and identify with them—to be one of them too. This, however, comes with a warning: some will criticize us and assume the worst. A friend of mine once spoke at a local church about his work with undocumented immigrants. At the end of his teaching, a visibly angry woman approached and asked for his full name. She told him she was going to report him for aiding and abetting criminals. She also had strong, condemning words for the pastor who invited him. Her strong response reveals the scandalous grace of Jesus.

But the scandal works both ways. Those who are looked on with suspicion often show us how deep the river of God's grace is. At the very moment we think we are giving God's grace it ends up coming back to us.

Jamie learned this not long ago. She had moved to Denver from the Midwest, only to find heartbreak, loneliness and financial difficulties surrounded her. In that place of darkness, alcohol and prescription drugs became good company, allowing her to forget her pain. It wasn't long before she hit bottom. With nowhere left to turn, she followed a friend to our church one night.

During that first church service, and the next five Sundays to follow, she could not hold back the tears. She did not know what was in store for her or what path to follow, but one thing she did know was that God found her. At one of those church services she heard about an opportunity to learn about homelessness, and for some reason, signed up.

The opportunity was not what she expected. Rather than sit and listen to someone talk about homelessness, she and others went for a walk in a Denver neighborhood that has a large homeless population. On this walk, she was given the opportunity to experience the life of a person who is homeless.

One exercise on the walk was to stand on a street corner holding a cardboard sign, reading "Anything helps." She fought this one, and said there was no way she was going to do it. After all, she was not homeless. More than that, she was wearing a Patagonia jacket, heels and a diamond ring. She tried to explain herself to those leading the walk, and said she felt she would be disrespecting the homeless. She quickly found her protest was getting her nowhere and was convinced to give it a try.

Within seconds of holding the cardboard sign, a man walked up

from behind and said, "Here." He placed something in her hand
and began to walk across the street. He was carrying a burger from
a fast food restaurant up the street, and what he had placed in her
hand was his change of $0.65. She ran after the man, yelling "Wait,
wait, no! You don't understand."

He turned, looked at her, smiled and said, "I don't need to understand; I am homeless too. God bless."

Tears streamed down Jamie's face, and by the time she got back
to the group leading the walk, she was sobbing. She fell into the
arms of a friend and explained what had happened. This man,
whom many looked at with suspicion, did not pass any judgment,
did not need to hear her story but welcomed her with open arms,
and was willing to help in any way he could.

In one instant, one homeless man acted as a window of grace,
and for the first time in years brought light to her darkness. As
she continued to cry, the dark truths about her past began to flood
out of her mouth. Jamie knew she was not so different from him.
That's how grace works. In giving it, we receive it, and learn we
all need it.

This is why grace blurs the lines and boundaries that bad religion
works so hard to maintain. Jesus upset the religious because he
never hung out with the right crowd. Even more, he was never
concerned about who people saw him with.

In fact, he often sought out the lowly, the vulnerable and those
trapped on the margins. More than just looking for them, he identified with them, he lived among them, and he sat with them. His
behavior and the crowds he chose to travel in upset the religious
norms of his day.

Some of the religious elite taught that sin was contagious. They
believed the clothing of the people Jesus ate with was unclean,
which means that if you touched their clothing, you would be considered unclean and cleansing would be required so you could once

again worship in the temple. Everything Jesus said and did worked against this teaching.

He believed *his* love, joy and hope were far more contagious than sin could ever be. *Amen.*

This is why he touched those who were unclean and they became clean. Jesus was not concerned that he was going to catch the sin they had, but he was confident that they would catch his forgiveness, grace and mercy. In doing this, he turned the social and religious order of his day on its head and brought freedom to those who had been enslaved by that order.

The religious who accused Jesus of being one of the sinners were overly concerned with legalistic regulations. They were wrapped up with having the right approach, obeying the right rules, possessing and defending their viewpoint, and enforcing those rules on others. By doing this, they gained the power and influence to judge others who stepped out of line.

What we see in the heart of Jesus is something different. He ignored the religious status quo. His concern was about standing *with* those who had been abused and dismissed by the religious elite with all of their regulations.

Jesus did not come to merely advocate for the rights of the poor, defend the cause of the outcast and speak up for sinners. No, he was poor, he joined the outcasts, and he became sin for them (2 Corinthians 5:21). He did this with such depth that he was identified as one of them. He did not just understand their shame; he took it on himself.

When they spoke of their pain, their hunger or their experience of oppression, Jesus was able to say, "I know," because he lived it with them. Jesus entered so deeply and so fully into their experience of hurting, being oppressed and being marginalized that he stood alongside them and bore their disgrace.

His presence among them showed them that, no matter how far

they felt from God, God was near to them—so close that he became one of them. Jesus' concern had nothing to do with what they could offer him. He never demanded they do all they could to get to him. We see in the person of Jesus, in the most scandalous of ways, God doing all he can to get to us. He still does.

The life of Jesus was caught up in sitting and dining and living among the sinners. This should give us great hope. Maybe you, because of the actions or words or beliefs of certain people, have been made to feel like a sinner, a glutton, a slut or a drunk. If that's the case, then know this: you are exactly the kind of person Jesus would love to have dinner with. He'd love to be called your friend.

This is what Paul was saying in the poem he recorded in his letter to the Philippians:

[Jesus] being in very nature God,
>   did not consider equality with God something to be used
>   to his own advantage;
rather, he made himself nothing
>   by taking the very nature of a servant,
>   being made in human likeness.
And being found in appearance as a man,
>   he humbled himself
>   by becoming obedient to death—
>   even death on a cross! (Philippians 2:6-8)

This is how fully and deeply Jesus has entered into our human experience: He has borne our disgrace and sorrow. He was willing to be displayed shamefully, naked and hanging on a cross. What can we say about a God like that? We know what Fronto and the graffiti artist thought. They believed this God was an ass.

I'd say that's good theology, because that is exactly what Jesus was willing to become so he could be with us and become one of us. More than that, it shows in Alexamanos the proper response to such a God. Rightfully so, he lifts up his hands and worships Jesus, and along with him, we should all raise our hands in worship to Jesus the Christ, Son of the living God—the one who became an ass for our salvation and for the redemption of the world.

what a great chapter

12

The New Fig Leaf

If you were the devil, in an effort to keep humanity away from the God who will do anything to get to his people, what would you do? How would you drown out the voice of God, calling, "Where are you?" I suspect that if you ran around like a mad man and told everyone to run and hide, they might be inclined not to listen. But what if you distracted humanity just enough so that they remained in hiding and never noticed? This just might work.

Several years ago a couple asked me to perform their wedding. We met together for the first time and they told me their story. They went back and forth, telling me about their families, where they were from and how they met. At one point the woman said to me, "I used to schedule appointments with my dad . . ."

I couldn't help but interrupt. I wanted to be sure I heard her right. "Did you say, 'I used to schedule appointments with my dad'?" I asked. Looking back I'm not sure I hid my surprise well at all because she laughed nervously, almost as if to say she did not mean to include that part of her story.

She explained that her dad bought her a smartphone when she was in high school so they could sync their schedules. This was necessary in his opinion; otherwise they might not see each other. I wondered what ever happened to sitting around the dinner table, going for a walk together, or turning off the television and being with your family. For some, these things seem to be an impossibility.

Then a few months ago, I was with a fellow who told me he is unable to do anything without having his phone, computer or a television nearby. He said he feels anxiety when he has to sit for twenty minutes and feed his three-month-old son if he cannot watch ESPN, check emails or read the news. He is not alone. We all know people who can't stop, and too often, *we* are those people.

Just a few weeks ago I was feeling worn out and stressed. Whenever I feel this way, I withdraw from everyone and everything. So one night I was at home, sitting in a chair in our living room, and my daughter was speaking to me while I stared at my phone. She finally said, "Dad you're not even listening to me. You're acting like I am not here!"

She was right—sort of. I wasn't so much acting like *she* wasn't there; I was pretending like *I* wasn't there. All I wanted to do was get away, not have to think and not have to be around people. For me, my phone is a way of escaping, even if just for a moment, so I don't have to think about the things that bring stress. I use it to hide.

Technology helps us do more things faster, yet we have less time than ever before. We have more devices to help us stay connected with others, yet we constantly grow more lonely and isolated. People are plugged in to their headphones, emailing, texting, tweeting, watching television, updating their Facebook statuses or doing anything to distract themselves. Of course, it all comes across quite innocently.

None of these things are especially wrong or sinful. In fact, they are just entertaining, but entertainment is something we have come to value because, the more entertained we are, the less we have to think—which allows us to remain hidden. No doubt, this sounds outrageous, but is it possible that this is happening? Why are we unable, or unwilling, to unplug from the noise? What outside of ourselves is driving us?

We may tell ourselves we are in a busy season, but if we're honest, we might recognize we have been busy for years. We will always need to reply to one more email, or broker one more deal, or squeeze in one more meeting. It's possible that we are not just in a busy season but we are addicted to staying busy. If we can stay busy, we won't have time to see our true selves. If we turn up the volume on the noise in our world, we won't be able to hear the still small voice of God, asking, "Where are you?"

The more we log on to connect, the more we remain disconnected from God and others, and the easier it is to live lives of self-deception without anyone knowing the real us—even ourselves. This frantic pace that we are trained to keep in our world may be the very thing destroying us. The philosopher Blaise Pascal is credited as saying, "All men's miseries derive from not being able to sit in a quiet room alone."

Unfortunately, in the moments we do try and connect, we don't do much better. Many people spend an hour or more each week attending worship gatherings in local churches. Some do this out of habit, but most take the time in hopes of connecting with God and others. The problem is: churches have become masters at keeping us busy too.

How many pastors' kids hate the church because their dads or moms are never home, never at their plays or games, because they are always working? Of course, the parents don't call it work; they call it ministry. Somehow this is supposed to make it more acceptable.

I met with the pastor of a church who demands his staff work a minimum of six days, or fifty-five hours, every week. He explained most of the people in their congregation work seven days a week and more than seventy hours, and he wants his church staff to earn the respect of their congregation. For them, busyness is a value.

When those who are leading the church think this way, we can see why religion has, for many, become about doing more. Church is just another event on our calendar to keep us busy. People are invited to volunteer, attend worship gatherings, participate in a Bible study, join a small group, go on a mission trip and serve their neighborhood. Those who do the most are the ones who often receive the most praise. We fill up our lives with more noise than we had before joining the church. This has become so normal that silence is no longer welcomed in many places.

Once, when I was guest-teaching at a church, toward the end of my teaching I had a time of silence for one minute. Afterward, many people wanted to speak with me to let me know how awful the silence was. Before the next service started, the pastor said to me, "We don't do 'dead air' here." Just sixty seconds of silence for them was a living hell.

When the noise is gone, we are laid bare. Silence rips the leaves off and pulls us out of hiding in a way nothing else does, and it brings us face to face with our naked selves. The thought of this can be terrifying. So rather than create silence, we create noise, keep churchgoers busy and allow them to stay hidden. Religion like this may just be the best trick the evil one has ever played on us. We feel like we are doing something good and getting closer to God, but in the end we may only be serving ourselves and moving further from him.

This way of living is exhausting and demoralizing because, no matter how hard we try, we are not getting any closer. Maybe this is why so many people burn out and end up resenting God and the church. They tried something they believed would lead them to God, but they ended up more lost than they were at the start. They never realized that the more they wandered around looking for God, the more lost they became—even when they were busy doing religion.

With all of this hiding going on, perhaps we should ask what has made us so fearful? Are we really scared of God, or perhaps, are we terrified of who we are? We know what lurks inside us. We are all too familiar with the thoughts rolling around in our heads and the feelings tumbling about in our hearts. We possess an insatiable desire to see ourselves in the best light possible and do all we can to be seen in this light.

Several weeks ago, on a warm spring afternoon, my wife and I sat together in our living room. We had the windows open and enjoyed the gentle breeze and the fresh smell of spring. Outside, our children played with kids from the neighborhood. They made up a game that was part Star Wars and part Swiss Family Robinson. All went well for them until one of them broke the rules they had just made up.

At this, one of my kids yelled, "No!" And then . . . it was on. An argument ensued between my kids and the neighborhood kids, and it was like listening to tribal warfare in its infantile stages. They accused and blamed, not caring about what the other had to say.

Then, as quickly as the fight erupted, it ended with one of the children screaming, "Fine! Then I won't play with you!"

The others responded in turn by yelling, "Fine!" Our gate opened as the neighborhood kids left, and our back door flew open as our children stormed inside.

My wife asked calmly, "Are you guys okay? What was going on out there?"

Without a moment's hesitation, my children launched into an explanation of what happened. The summary was this: they were completely right, and the other children were completely wrong and horribly unfair.

Unfortunately for them, we had heard the entire argument while sitting in our living room. As we listened to their explanation, we knew nothing our children told us was even remotely true. Their story was not just one-sided; it was totally false. After they finished telling us their version of the events that unfolded outside, my wife said, "Your dad and I heard the whole fight, and what you told us isn't what really happened, is it?"

Unmoved by this revelation, they looked us right in the eye and said, "Yes! That's exactly what happened."

As I looked at them, I realized they really believed they told us the truth. In their minds they did not lie to us at all. In a matter of minutes they had gone from fighting with their friends to telling a story they believed was true. As I watched my children then, it was like watching myself—the practice of self-deception.

Few things are worse than coming to grips with who we are, what we have done or what really happened. We tell ourselves a story of what we wish we had done or what we would have wanted to happen, and in doing so, we lie to ourselves. We hide our true selves behind these stories so we can pretend we are the person we have always wanted to be. But there are times when we discover who we are, and it is painful. We see this in the story of Peter denying Jesus.

Peter's denial of Jesus wasn't just a polite way of deceiving those who asked him the questions. Peter used the strongest, legal language possible to insist he had no idea who Jesus was. None of this came as any surprise to Jesus. He told Peter he was going to deny him not once but three times.

Peter refused to believe him. He told Jesus that even if all of his friends abandoned him, Peter himself would not. He even went so far as to tell Jesus that, if he had to die with him, he would do so. Then, just a few hours later, Peter did as Jesus predicted. He denied having any knowledge of who Jesus was. The moment Peter did this, Jesus turned and looked straight at him (Luke 22:61). Peter remembered Jesus' prediction, was overcome and wept bitterly.

His reaction was not just regret or remorse. He was overcome—like a ship on a raging sea, filling with water. Something inside Peter shattered to pieces. Exactly what caused this emotion? Peter's response seemed to be about far more than simple regret. He had made mistakes before but had never responded with such emotion. What caused him such pain that he wept like he did?

Perhaps, for Peter, it was the first time he came face to face with who he had been all along. The mask he had worked so hard to keep up had shattered, and he was confronted with his broken soul—one capable of walking away from and denying Jesus. His tears were the result of seeing who he really was without the fig leaves on.

Before this moment Peter was wrapped in the belief that he was who he wanted to be. He was able to confidently tell Jesus he'd be with him to the death. Peter was so sure of this that he didn't believe he was lying; he really believed his words to be true. This all crumbled when he denied Jesus. One might say something died in him that day—like the lies he told himself about the person he wanted to be.

This kind of death is painful, but there is no other way. Every journey begins where we are, not where we hope to be or where we wish we were. This first step is the most difficult because it demands honesty. When we admit we are not the person we want to be or pretend to be, something has to die.

This is the very thing Jesus talked about when he invited all who would follow him to pick up their crosses, deny themselves and lose their lives (Mark 8:34-35). Paul shared this message in his letter to the church in Ephesus. He reminded them of the self-deceived way they used to live. According to Paul, this is not the way to live any longer, which is why he told them to "put off your old

self" (Ephesians 4:22). He went a step further in his letter to the
Colossian church, where he told them to "put to death" the old self
(Colossians 3:5).

This is strong and violent language. We are to kill, shoot,
bludgeon, drown, strangle, suffocate or stab the old self—whatever
we have to do to be sure we have killed it. When the old self comes
knocking, we must destroy it because it is not welcome anymore.
We cannot live any longer by covering ourselves in leaves and
hiding in lies. That is the old self. It is the mask we wear to make
ourselves and others think we are someone different, and if we hold
on to it forever, it will kill us.

The old self is like the fig leaves the man and the woman used to
hide their fear and their nakedness. The leaves cover the real us.
They are full of lies, lead us away from God's love and invite us to
travel on the path of sin. This is the self we are to kill. The problem
is that we are too busy to notice we are wearing leaves and hiding.
Worse yet, in the moments when we do see a glimpse of who we
are, we run away.

Maybe the first step *before* the first step is to stop and consider
the question, "Where are you?" If we continue moving, we will only
get more lost. Like Peter, we must come face to face with who and
where we really are—even if we have to weep bitter tears. Seeing
ourselves without the fig leaves is painful, and removing them feels
like death.

Of course, this is good news! Because death is just the beginning.
As the leaves come off, our new self, the person we truly are, comes
to life. In that very place, we discover our new life and our new
name. This is no small thing. A name is not just a simple way you
are known. A name speaks of who you are and reflects your identity.
I once witnessed the power a new name brings with it.

⊕

Our church had a baptism service, during which several of those being baptized were deeply emotional. I learned that some of those who were to be baptized chose new names. They had been raised in a difficult and violent world, and they had recently experienced the death of their old selves. They were not the same; for in their death, they were given new life in Jesus. Their old names wouldn't do anymore. What better time to receive a new name than baptism?

In baptism we identify with Jesus in his death, burial and resurrection. We go under the water—buried in the likeness of his death—then we come out of the water—raised in the likeness of his resurrection. We hear this in Paul's letter to the church in Rome. He wrote, "Don't you know that all of us who were baptized into Christ Jesus were baptized into his death?" (Romans 6:3). He didn't stop there. He reminded them that death is just the beginning. "Just as Christ was raised from the dead . . . we too may live a new life" (Romans 6:4).

This is exactly what a new name is: new life. The trick is it only comes after death. Too many of us only want the resurrection, and we fail to see that, if this is going to happen, something or someone has to die. This is the struggle. Death is the tearing away the old so the new has a place to grow. Through this, we discover our new name that tells us who we are as much-loved daughters and sons of God. No longer do we have to live in hiding—no more fig leaves, distracting ourselves or pretending to be someone we are not. We have been found by the God we are looking for.

This is the beginning of a new life of freedom. We can stand with confidence, knowing we are holy.

Maybe that seems like a stretch.

Holy?

On most days we feel like a lot of things, but holy is not always one of them. However, what if we had the eyes to see ourselves as God sees us? It may help to rewind a few thousand years to a small, young church in a city named Colossae in Asia so we can answer that question. The apostle Paul wrote them a letter we now call Colossians, and when the church received the letter, they would have gathered together and heard the letter read aloud.

This would have been quite an interesting gathering in Colossae because, in the audience that day, was an escaped slave named Onesimus. The economy of the Roman Empire was built on the back of slaves, and according to the laws of his day, Onesimus was a fugitive. If slaves ran away, financial hardship would come to many, so when a slave did run away, they were severely punished to serve as a deterrent to others who might try the same thing.

Sitting in the room with the fugitive Onesimus was Philemon—Onesimus's slave master. He could have done anything he wanted to him, as masters were known to beat runaways, brand them with a hot iron and even kill them. I cannot imagine what the tension was like in the room when they gathered to hear Paul's words. Did they greet one another? Did Philemon invite some friends who were on his side? How many people took the time to point out that Onesimus, the fugitive, was finally back?

Paul began his letter by writing, "To God's holy people in Colossae" (Colossians 1:2). How would Onesimus and Philemon have felt when they heard Paul call them *holy*? A fugitive is holy? A slave master who could destroy another person's life is holy?

How would you have felt if you were there and heard Paul call *you* holy? What if, the day before, you and your spouse had a major fight and you said horrible things to each other? What if you had been looking at porn the night before? What if you had just swindled someone in a business deal? When you heard the words, "God's holy people," you may have thought he was not speaking to you.

But he was speaking to you. He was speaking to all who were there, and he is speaking to us today. In six of his letters to different churches, Paul addressed the people as *holy*. His words are a statement of fact. He offers no clarifying comments as to who is and who is not holy. Too often we think of holiness as something we have to achieve. We think we have to do certain religious things, behave better or learn more theology. Nothing could be further from the truth. Through the death and resurrection of Jesus, we have new life and are made holy. This means we are set apart to God for his special purposes.

We are separate, withheld from the ordinary. To be holy is to tap into the majesty of God. God set the people of Israel apart when he called them to live as a holy nation. They were not an ordinary nation, but ones through whom God would bring the redemption of the world. The same was said of the temple; it was no ordinary building. Peter brings these images together in his letter to the church when he said we "are living stones God is building into his spiritual temple" and we are a "holy nation, God's very own possession" (1 Peter 2:5, 9 NLT). Wait, we are God's temple?

Temples were platforms for the divine rule and reign of a king over his kingdom on this earth. They were sacred places where heaven and earth came together. Now Peter tells us *we* are the temple of God on this earth. *We* are the place where God's rule and reign is present, the very place God dwells.

With Jesus we are set apart to reclaim what God intended when the man and the woman worked and cared for God's good creation. We are free to participate with God in making his kingdom a reality on earth as it is in heaven. We are invited to work alongside him, and rediscover what it means to live fully and freely as those who bear his image. This is the new reality Jesus spoke about. He invited humanity to learn what it means to live as free men and women.

This brings us back to the question of how we see ourselves. What if we understood that we have been set apart and connected to the divine to show others what God is like? What if, when people were with us, they had a deep, abiding sense that God was in their midst? This kind of living could change everything.

Many of us find this so hard to believe because we lack the vision to see ourselves the way God sees us. In his eyes, we are set apart to actively work with him to restore and renew his good creation, just like the first man and woman. God's love invites us into the freedom of being fully alive as human beings again. We have the opportunity and responsibility as his image bearers to work with him, which then raises the question, what are we waiting for?

With every word we speak, every act we perform, every gift we give, we have an opportunity to represent God to others. Maybe all we need is to see who we already are—to see ourselves as God sees us and remove the fig leaves we are still wearing.

If we do this, we could participate with Jesus to bring a tangible sense of God's kingdom here on earth, just like it is in heaven. Of course, we will have to spend the rest of our lives learning what this looks like, but this is exactly what Jesus wanted. It's why he said, "Follow me."

13

And It Goes Like This

Standing over his casket was not easy. I had performed funerals before, but this was different. This guy was a few years younger than I was. These are not the kind of people that are supposed to die. When the graveside service concluded, the family stayed as they lowered the casket into the ground, and I felt like I was staring my death in the face. It was more than unsettling; I was downright scared.

Driving home after the funeral, I could not shake how uncomfortable I was. All kinds of questions rolled around in my head about whether I was wasting the years of my life, and if, when I one day died, people would say my life made a difference. As I wrestled with these questions, something struck me. As difficult as that funeral was, my greatest fear was not death. My greater fear was to consider my life and how I was living it. Standing over that grave did not bring me face to face with death; it brought me face to face with my life.

Nearly all people want to live a good life and know that the world is better because they lived. All of us want to believe that when we breathe our last breath, we will do so knowing that we have lived a life that mattered. At the same time, asking ourselves questions as to whether this is true of us is terrifying. Death forces us to answer the disturbing question Rabbi Harold Kushner asks, "Would our disappearance leave the world poorer, or just less crowded?" (*When All You've Ever Wanted Isn't Enough*, p. 19).

Within 120 years of me writing these words, every person who is living on this earth right now will be dead. While this is not exactly something you'd put on a greeting card with a picture of a cute rabbit hopping across a field of green grass, it's true. We will all be dead, and this means you too. One day, family and friends will surround you as they lay your body into the ground. They will cover the place with dirt, and set up a headstone, forever marking that spot in the earth where you will, at last, return to dust. In that moment they will say something about you. The question is, "What will they say?"

Will you or I have lived a life that mattered or will our lives have been wasted? The good news is we get a say in how these questions are answered.

When Jesus walked the earth, he lived a life that mattered and spoke about how all people could do the same. This message of hope was his gospel. Jesus said he came so that we could "have life, and have it to the full" (John 10:10).

Jesus was concerned about life here and now. His gospel was the good news that we can live fully in this world. That is why, when we limit the gospel to something that is a secure down payment for entrance into heaven when we die, we may just hold to a gospel other than Jesus'. If our central concern is finding life after death, there is a chance we will not find life before death.

A gospel that focuses on our death gets us ready to die, but Jesus' gospel gets us ready to live. The gospel of Jesus claims that, through his death, burial and resurrection, he brought a new reality to bear in this world, and he brought the liberation and forgiveness of sin that humanity so desperately needed. For those who receive Jesus' gospel, we have to learn a new way of thinking, living and seeing.

This is necessary because we have adapted to a way of life other than the life Jesus offers. To understand this, we need to go back again to the time when the first man and the first woman sinned. They were saddled with sorrow, anxiety and grief, and were forever banished from Eden. Could you imagine the look on Adam and Eve's faces, or their conversation when they first left the Garden?

I think of Dorothy in the *Wizard of Oz* after the tornado. She walked around with a bewildered look on her face, and said to her dog, Toto, "We're not in Kansas anymore." From the moment the man and the woman recognized they were naked, they knew deep inside that they were not in Eden anymore. They were in a brand new world, one wracked with sin and pain and death. Over time, however, they adapted. All humanity has done the same ever since.

As humans we are good at adapting quickly to almost any environment. We have grown comfortable outside of Eden. It has become our new normal. We have adapted to a world where we do not need to love God or others. We believe we can find love apart from God, and it even seems to work sometimes. We have become at home in a place far from Eden. But God was not going to let his good creation and humanity go so easily.

God did all he could to get to us, and because of Jesus, we no longer have to adapt to life outside of Eden. We can learn to live in a new way. This was Jesus' constant invitation when he said, "Repent." Too often, this word has been connected to the horrible phrase, "Turn or burn!" But this is not what Jesus was saying. The call to repentance is central to his message. It is not a threat but an invitation to be free.

Repentance speaks of changing our loyalty and completely reorienting the way we think about life. It means to stop going, thinking and living one way, and start going, thinking and living the opposite way. We must reclaim the message of Jesus, and proclaim not only the need for repentance but also the beauty of its message. Repentance is the call from our Father to come home. It invites us to experience the story of love, acceptance and reunion. It asks us to reorient our lives, to turn around, to stop going further from home and to answer the question, "Where are you?"

The Hebrew word for *repent* means "to turn," and the Greek word means "reorientation." This idea contained in Scripture is more than just a decision of the mind; it is a radical departure from the life we were living. It is not just about charting a new course on the same old map; it is about throwing out the old map altogether.

Jesus' gospel calls us to a radical reorientation of how we live on this earth. This is something we need to *learn* how to do. It's not just that heaven awaits us when we die but a whole new reality awaits us here and now. And we are all invited to participate in this new life. Much like when the people of Israel left Egypt and were no longer slaves, they had to learn how to live as free men and women. Like them, we must learn how to move from enslavement to freedom.

If we fail to learn how to live from Jesus, we are in danger of living in a new kind of slavery.

Make no mistake, we have been liberated in and through the death of Jesus, and are free to take off the leaves and come out of hiding. But too often we end up putting the leaves back on and wandering back into the bushes. One of the reasons this happens is because we have never been taught how to live freely as God's liberated people.

This is one reason true freedom is not always associated with Jesus or Christianity. Often we stress right behavior and strict adherence to lists of rules. The problem, of course, is our ability to obey long lists of rules often has little to do with the state of our hearts. Rather, rules just give us a way to define who we are and to separate ourselves from others. Those who live this way do not seem to be interested in freedom.

I once heard a preacher say, "I told my children that I prayed every day, 'God, if my children wander away from you, please remove them and take them home to be with you.'" He proudly went on to claim that all his children were "walking with the Lord." Never mind they were terrified of the other option. Is that a free life?

The very thing this preacher talked about is the same kind of thing I heard from people throughout my life. Everywhere I went I had a deep belief God was waiting to find me doing something wrong, and when he did, he would destroy my soul. My fear was massive because I knew God would not have to wait long to find me behaving badly.

Anytime I messed up, the thought of an angry God drove me to panicked repentance. I knew what God did to sinners, and I was certain God would get me somehow for what I had done. I was locked in a vicious cycle; as soon as I begged for forgiveness, it seemed like I was making my next mistake. I was not free. I was enslaved by fear.

My way of thinking reflects the widespread belief that God is angry and waiting to destroy sinful humans. He is like a brutal slave driver, ready to beat us whenever we do not obey his command. This belief is seen when devastation and disasters befall us here on earth and some religious leader claims God is punishing us. With events like 9/11 or the earthquake in Haiti, certain religious leaders pronounced these were the direct result of God's wrath. They even blamed specific groups of people for God's decision to allow these disasters to strike.

Belief in a God like this makes us into slaves, and it makes God out to be a harsh slave master. We are still enslaved to the lie that tells us we have to do everything in our power to appease him. While many are terrified of a God like this, there really is no reason to be scared at all, because a slave-master God like this is weak and easily manipulated and controlled. He is only stirred or calmed by our actions, which makes our relationship with him easy. We can live in certainty and know the outcomes of our actions well ahead of time. Perhaps this is why so many have devoted themselves to this kind of god: even though it commits them to a life of slavery, it allows them to be in control.

However, Jesus invites us into a brand new life of freedom, not a different kind of slavery. Often, freedom presents a greater challenge for us than slavery. Jesus knew this, which is why his plan was for us to be his disciples. Those who lived in the first-century world knew exactly what this meant: a disciple is a student, but not as we typically think of one.

In our context a student is a person who sits at a desk and writes down what the teacher puts up on his or her PowerPoint presentation so that they can spit it back out on a test. Students compile information but disciples pursue transformation.

This can be hard for us to grasp in our modern Western culture. And not just because of how we understand what it means to be a student, but also because of what it means to be a Christian. What Jesus was speaking of is not religious obligation, an increase in church attendance or more ritual. He was speaking about a way of life.

For many Christians, what is central to their faith is not a way of living but an event. That event happens in thousands of church buildings every Sunday morning all over our world. We commonly call it "church."

This event has become so central to the faith of many Christians that, today, many seminaries train pastors, and a great deal of their education is directed toward their efforts on Sunday mornings. In churches across America, the staff structure, their time and their energy is weighted toward creating an event for people to attend. All of this is puzzling because what other part of our week is anything like what we experience on a Sunday morning?

Where else do we regularly gather in a room with other people, many of whom we have never met, and burst into song? How often do we sit down in a chair facing a stage and sit idly, listening to someone talk for more than thirty minutes? What many of us experience on a Sunday morning may be a normal part of our week, but it is nothing like anything else we experience during our week. Is it any wonder why so many say, "I struggle to live out my faith"?

This idea of faith as an event is so ingrained in our minds that, when we hear Jesus' call to be a disciple, we begin to wonder if we can find the time to fit that into our schedule. What we fail to realize is that Jesus is not interested in whether or not we can find a place for him in our calendar; he wants our entire calendar so he can teach us how to live in it.

Somehow we have turned the message of Jesus on its head. My friend Mike frequently says, "We believe that we should build the church so that we can make disciples, but Jesus said to make disciples and you will build the church." If we are to be disciples, then, we must recognize that following Jesus is not something we schedule; it is a lifestyle. It's not about doing more; it's learning how to see, hear and think differently. Which may very well lead us to the place where we find we can actually do less.

In Jesus' day, disciples learned a new way of living from teachers they called rabbis. When a rabbi called a disciple to learn from him, he would say, "Follow me." These words were an invitation to learn from him, to imitate him and to carve out a new life on earth. But they were also a statement about the disciple. A rabbi would never invite a disciple to follow him unless he thought the disciple could become like him. And if a disciple responded to a call from a rabbi, they placed their full trust in him to teach them a better way of life. They knew their current way of life was not what they wanted anymore, so they would do all they could to imitate the life of the rabbi. The goal was to imitate their rabbi so well that they would begin to resemble him.

The rabbi would begin by teaching his disciples about his understanding of God, his interpretation of the Bible, and about how he lived his everyday life. They would engage in questions and responses, and the disciples would learn why the rabbi lived the way he did. Much of this teaching was done in the midst of everyday life. The rabbi would go about his day, and the disciples would watch him.

Over the course of time, the rabbi would ask the disciples to help him with certain things he had to do. Eventually the disciples would be asked to do what they had seen their rabbi do, and he would help them. Then the day would come when they would be sent to do all they had learned, and the rabbi would watch them do it. D - Cycles

When we consider the life of Jesus, we see over and over a life defined by love, mercy, grace, justice, compassion, hope and joy. Jesus wanted his disciples to learn from him, imitate him, act like him and think like him. He wanted them to be his presence, his hands, his feet and his voice in this world. That is why he told them to go and make disciples, to teach all people "in the practice of all I have commanded you" (Matthew 28:20 *The Message*). Jesus was telling his disciples that he believed they were enough like him to teach others how to be like him. It's no different for us.

Jesus' command was simple. He expected his disciples to go and teach others how to take on his way of life. Of course, his disciples were imperfect and flawed, and would never be exactly like Jesus, but this did not seem to concern him. He believed they could do it. More than that, Jesus told them they would do greater things than he did (John 14:12), and Jesus has given us the same invitation.

We are imperfect and flawed too. Like Paul, we may look at ourselves and think "what a wretched man I am" (Romans 7:24). But Jesus' call to us is the same: we are to teach others in the practice of all he commanded. Regardless of what you may think of yourself, Jesus seems to think we can do greater things than him. Maybe this is why Paul, who thought himself to be wretched, could also say, "Follow my example, as I follow the example of Christ" (1 Corinthians 11:1).

Jesus invites us to learn his way of life, which is life to the full. This is his good news. When we respond to this gospel, we agree to learn how to live like Jesus, to be his hope-filled presence on this earth and to actively participate with God in his renewal and salvation of the world.

Which brings us to a question of faith. Do we trust Jesus enough to do life his way, or will we insist on continuing to adapt outside of Eden?

The question of trust in Jesus is central to the life of a disciple. It means no longer trusting him only with our deaths but also with our lives. It is the belief that, no matter how much we think we know or can do or how capable we believe ourselves to be, we recognize that imitating him and learning about this new life is far better. This is much easier said than done because this kind of life takes immense faith.

There are a lot of times in my life when I am tempted to believe I do not need to learn from Jesus because I am getting along just fine. Admittedly, I see myself as a somewhat capable person. I realize this sounds horribly arrogant, but it's true. There are so many times when I don't trust Jesus like I should. It's not always about a big thing either, which makes it easier for me to think I should go on adapting.

There are times when I believe I do not need any help being a good father; or moments when I think I have the pastor thing nailed down and am doing well at my job; days when I find more security in what I can earn, save and spend than in the daily bread God faithfully gives. These are the times when I choose to adapt and not truly live.

The invitation of Jesus to me is to repent from my attitude of self-sufficiency and trust him with my life. This seems like a lot to handle, and it can seem daunting to think about learning how to live like Jesus in our world. We can convince ourselves we don't have what it takes. If that's how you feel, then you are in the perfect place to hear the good news of Jesus.

He invited anyone who would come to be his disciple, saying, "Come to me, all you who are weary and burdened, and I will give you rest. . . . Learn from me, for I am gentle and humble in heart, and you will find rest for your souls" (Matthew 11:28-29).

Eugene Peterson translated these verses in *The Message* as, "Are you tired? Worn out? Burned out on religion? Come to me. Get away with me and you'll recover your life. I'll show you how to take a real rest. Walk with me and work with me—watch how I do it. Learn the unforced rhythms of grace." Does this sound like good news?

Becoming a disciple of Jesus is not about doing enough to earn the right to follow him. It is about trusting that God has already done enough, so we can follow Jesus, learn from him and imitate his life here and now. This faith in him will one day lead us to the place where we spend this life, and the next, in right relationship with God—because we have been found by him.

Jesus' good news causes us to have to reframe the question about getting to heaven. If we trust God in this life enough to repent and become a disciple of Jesus, why would we live any differently after we die? If we are embraced by God and embrace him in this life, then we can expect the same in the life to come.

This is good news indeed, but not for everyone. This good news is a threat to the evil one. He wants to keep us out of Eden. His lies tell us that adapting is the best we can hope for. The more we proclaim the good news, the more of a fight we can expect.

Jesus didn't say living as a disciple would be easy, but he did say the gates of hell could not prevent him from establishing his kingdom here on earth. God has found us, and we have the joy of joining him in his search for all people. There is a fight to be had, but it may not be the kind of fight you would expect—because the enemy is not who you think it is.

14

Lay Down Your Guns

Shortly before my father turned twelve, he and his sister roller-skated in a park near their home in Havana, Cuba. A black box truck pulled up and parked near the presidential palace, but they did not notice it. Suddenly, people poured out of the truck, and the sound of gunfire and exploding grenades rang out. The date was March 13, 1957, and the now infamous attack on the presidential palace had begun.

My dad and his sister fell to the ground, crawled under a marble bench and cowered in fear. To their terror the gunfire grew louder as those who attacked the palace retreated into the park where the two hid. The presidential guard fired on the attackers, and they fired back. A bullet hit the bench a few feet from them, and they crouched lower. The noise was deafening. They were not just caught in the middle of a firefight; they were caught in the age-old, violent story of empires.

My father was born in Cuba and lived there until he was fifteen. A few years after he was born, Fulgencio Batista seized political power by force, staging a coup. Over time some grew weary of his rule and planned violence against him. This response was exactly what came about through Fidel Castro. His stated intent was to pursue justice and rid Cuba of corruption. As noble as his intentions sounded, he only ended up repeating the cycle of violence that

Batista was guilty of. The actions of Batista and Castro reflect a powerful myth, which teaches that violence will bring peace.

The story of my father's country is another example that reminds us this is never the case. Violence never has and will never bring about peace. In the case of Cuba, a violent dictator was ousted by a violent revolution that many supported. This is the story of nearly every empire in the history of the earth. They have begun and ended the same way—with violence and bloodshed. Generations come and go, and eventually the empire experiences a decline, and a new empire rises up, wanting to gain independence or expand its territory. The new empire attacks, the old empire falls, and the new one takes its place. When the fighting is done, the now-mighty empire reaps the *temporary* rewards of its violence—a time of prosperity.

While this is the common story among humanity, we cannot forget that God's ways are not ours. He did not establish his kingdom in the normal way. Make no mistake, Jesus brought about his kingdom through bloodshed and violence, but it was done *to* him not *by* him.

 So if Jesus brought the kingdom of God here on this earth through his suffering, then why would we think we could do it any other way? The call of Jesus was to imitate him, to be his disciple. In Jesus, we see the ultimate picture of God doing all he can to get to us. As those who have joined with God in his search for all people, we must do it his way. This means we must be willing to suffer and even lose our lives for the sake of the kingdom.

Of course, this may sound ridiculous. If you want to bring about a kingdom, you need to stand up for your rights and be sure to let others know who has the power. But this is only true for earthly empires, not for the kingdom of heaven. Of course, this doesn't mean God is not interested in reclaiming this world and restoring his kingdom, but rather, he just didn't plan on doing so in the conventional way of empires. When Jesus lived on this earth, he displayed what it looks like for a king to bring freedom, liberation and a kingdom without the normal use of violence or force. Jesus was meek.

A meek person is one who approaches life and the world with tremendous humility, the kind of person whose ultimate aim is not his or her benefit. Rather the meek seek the highest and greatest good for all people—even if the greatest good comes at their expense. The meek are those who have the capacity to participate with Jesus in bringing about his kingdom.

One of the greatest pictures of meekness I ever have witnessed was a young woman named Angela. She was born in Mozambique and was a child of privilege. Her parents had enough money to send her to the best schools. She excelled as a student and received an academic scholarship to an American university. While studying in the United States, she had opportunities to pursue a singing career. Her voice is one of the most beautiful I have ever heard. She had every door open to her to pursue the path of wealth, fame and success, but she never stepped through any of them. Instead, after she received her college degree and her master's degree, she returned home.

When I met her, we were in the shack of a man dying from AIDS. He had contracted the disease from a prostitute, and later gave the disease to his wife, who died as a result. He could not handle the thought of having been responsible for his wife's death. One night, unable to cope, he got drunk, returned home and sexually assaulted his adult daughter. This horrible act gave his daughter AIDS too.

Angela was sitting on the ground next to this man, holding his hand. Every time she spoke to him, her words oozed with tenderness and love. After spending time in conversation with him, she got up and cleaned his shack. She wasn't just dusting but was cleaning everything, including his urine and feces. All the while, she did not wear rubber gloves.

I asked her later why she was not protecting herself better, and she explained that, if she wore gloves, she would be telling him he had AIDS. Even though everyone, including him, knew he had AIDS, no one would say it, because to do so would mean that he was already dead. She did not wear gloves because she wanted to tell this man he was loved. She could have had the American dream; instead she embraced meekness.

It's no wonder Jesus called the meek "blessed" and said they would "inherit the earth" (Matthew 5:5). This is a deep, abiding truth that points to the heart of what meekness is. Those who are meek are not trying to get, grasp or gain something. Rather they are willing to give everything up for the sake of others. And because they stand empty-handed, they are able to receive.

This is explicit in Jesus' words. The meek inherit God's good gift; they do not take it. This describes the difference between kingdom and empire. Empires have demands, have expectations and operate with a sense of entitlement. Those of us living in the empire are taught to believe it is our responsibility to get what we want.

We spend our time clawing our way to the top. We amass wealth and possessions, and tell ourselves the lie that we have worked to get all we have—and, therefore, that we deserve all we have. God spoke to this kind of attitude. He reminded his people that, if they believed they earned everything by the work of their hands, they would become arrogant and forget God had given it to them.

We must heed this warning. Otherwise, we run the risk of becoming like the citizens of Sodom. The sins of Sodom were that they were "arrogant, overfed and unconcerned," and "they did not help the poor and needy" (Ezekiel 16:49). Imagine a world where those who amassed wealth became consumed with amassing more. What would it be like to live in a country where the wealthy openly asked questions about what they really owed to the unemployed, the vulnerable, the poor and the "have-nots"? Unfortunately, this is not a difficult question to answer.

We do not have to look far to see those in places of privilege and power who are indifferent to the needs of the poor and marginalized. This attitude is the product of those who believe they have worked hard to get what they have. They forget one thing: they did not get what they possess; all they have was given to them.

The meek understand this. No longer do they have to fight, pursue, achieve or attain. They have discovered the joy in working alongside Jesus with open hands, gratefully receiving anything he gives them. When we live meekly, we no longer ask questions of how much of our possessions or cash we should give. We ask how much of God's gifts should we keep (Tom Sine, *The New Conspirators*, p. 247).

To live meekly is to live freely. From this place we are able to pursue justice and long for the kingdom to be a deeper reality here on earth. We live with a willingness to give all we have received to see this happen. For we know that, even in the times we experience loss, it was never ours to begin with.

Few people have embodied this kind of selfless, free life more than Martin Luther King Jr. He was willing to give everything for the cause of justice. He and his wife, Coretta, spoke of the day when he would be forced to give his life, knowing he would one day be killed. They recognized the highest and greatest good was not saving his life, but as he said in his famous "I Have a Dream" speech, giving up everything to see "the sons of former slaves and the sons of former slave owners" sit "together at the table of brotherhood" (www.archives.gov/press/exhibits/dream-speech.pdf, p. 4).

His desire was not to topple the oppressor through violent means.

He wanted the best for all people, including the oppressor, because he knew they too were enslaved in a different way. He was not interested in his side conquering the other side. His deep desire was to see the love of God appeal to the hearts and minds of the oppressor.

To overcome, to bring God's kingdom, Dr. King imitated Jesus in his meekness. He allowed himself to suffer, be jailed and, ultimately, be killed. He sought the greatest good for all people, and he was able to do this because he knew who the real enemy was. We might identify those who participate in the evil of racism as the enemy, but the real enemy is far more evil and much more powerful.

I'm not sure what comes to your mind when you hear the word *enemy*. For me, one especially clear autumn morning in 2001 is what instantly pops into my head. On that day, Americans understood enmity in a way we had never experienced before. The events of 9/11 will be forever etched in the minds of those who experienced them. Every anniversary since that fateful day, I have been asked where I was when I heard the news. Like everyone else, I will never forget it.

I was in Grand Rapids, Michigan, and had just walked out of a seminary classroom after a Hebrew class. A fellow student named Dan looked panicked and asked if we heard about the plane that had flown into the World Trade Center in New York. Minutes later, as I was driving and listening to the radio, I will never forget hearing the voice say in disbelief, "Oh my God, oh my God, oh my God . . . one of the towers is falling. The south tower just collapsed." I could not believe what I heard.

I had stood at the foot of those monstrous buildings. They stood far above all the other buildings and defined the south end of the New York City skyline. How could one of them have fallen? Minutes later the second tower collapsed. Like most Americans, I watched and rewatched the footage of those towers falling. On that day, no one knew how many people died but we knew we had witnessed a massive loss of human life.

Within the next few days, the world learned about a plot that had been in the works for years. We learned about a relatively small, extremist organization, falsely wearing the badge of religion, that planned the attacks of 9/11 in meticulous detail. They hated us and wanted to destroy everything we held dear: we were their enemy.

Many in the United States felt the same way and wanted to destroy them: they were our enemy. The United States responded with swift and aggressive military action. When we did, I recall few who were opposed to finding and killing those who were responsible for what the world witnessed on that clear, blue autumn day. We wanted them dead. On the surface it was a battle of ideals, religions and nations. The United States had been attacked, and we retaliated. But that is not really what happened.

As awful as that day was, what we witnessed was not a violent act done, ultimately, against us. Nor was our retaliation and military aggression a counterattack against them. The truth is we are much like those who masterminded the heinous events of 9/11. We like to think we are different from them. We tell ourselves that, no matter what we may do in response, it's not as bad as what they have done. The problem is that none of this is true.

As much as we like to draw dividing lines of hostility, those boundaries will only ever be our own creation. We all stand on the same side of the dividing line of hostility, opposed to Jesus himself. In his letter to the Colossian church, Paul claimed humanity was the enemy of Jesus because of our evil behavior. In the same way, in Paul's letter to the church in Rome, he reminded them they were God's enemies. This is strong language. All we can expect from an enemy is hostility, hatred and danger. *Enemy* goes beyond negative feelings or the inability to get along. An enemy is one who, if given the chance, would kill us. And if the chance never came, he would create one so he could. This is how Paul describes our relationship toward God.

As for me, I'm not sure I like this. I'd like to think that God and I have always been on decent terms. Even in the moments when I have wandered from him, I can't say I've entertained thoughts of destroying him. So an enemy of God? Sounds a little harsh.

But being an enemy of God makes complete sense if we are able to see that whatever we do to one another is actually something we do to God himself. Just as Jesus said, whatever we do for the least of his brothers and sisters we do to him (Matthew 25:40). So it is with being an enemy of God: whatever we do against others we do to God.

As much as it hurts us to have things done against us, God is, in fact, the real victim. As good as it feels to seek revenge or retaliate against those we call our enemies, those actions make God bleed. Whatever evil we do to another person, we do it to God. All of us—you, me, the people we like the least, the men who flew planes into buildings—are enemies of God.

The Gospels speak of the day Jesus was crucified. One of his disciples betrayed him, another one denied even knowing him, and the rest ran away to save their skin. Some of the priests and religious elite wanted to find a reason to kill him and they finally did. The Romans were the ones who nailed him to a cross and executed him. While he hung there, some passed by, mocked him and laughed at him.

Jesus was alone.

In the blood, torture and violence of Jesus' crucifixion, humanity is confronted with the depths of our enmity, hostility and hatred of God. We see our toxic words, our hateful thoughts, our murderous acts and our lust for revenge in the bleeding, suffering, crucified Christ. On the cross we see a picture of God absorbing all cruel, evil, sinful human actions ever done. This includes those things we have done and those things done to us. We can no longer distance ourselves from others, thinking we are different. We must change the way we see others, which means changing the side on which we stand.

There are always two sides to the cross—enmity and love. We were on the side of enmity, but Jesus was on the side of grace and love. When Paul says we were God's enemies, he never says God was our enemy. Hostility between God and us was one way. We directed our hate toward God; it was not from him toward us. God's response to our enmity is love—love so intense and so bewildering that, while we were his enemies, he died for us. God has never been against us; he has always been for us.

In the same way that we can see our hostility in the violence of the cross, so we can also see our pain, shame, sin and guilt in the beaten and bruised body of Jesus. Some of us have painful memories of wounds we received that are so deep we cannot fully explain how we felt, or still feel. Others of us know people in this world who, when their names are mentioned, we still feel a twinge of pain all these years later. Many of us have had our heart broken by someone we loved, or someone we trusted betrayed us.

This is the kind of deep pain, the kind we cannot put words to, that we see embodied in the suffering Jesus on the cross. When words fail to describe the agony we've endured, we can look at the cross. There we see Jesus, bruised, battered, naked, bleeding and dying, and we are reminded that as much as we were his enemies, he is for us. This allows us to cease living in hostility toward him and toward others, and to live for him and for others. For Jesus said whatever we do out of love, mercy and compassion for his brothers and sisters, it's as though we have done it to him.

When we see our world this way, we will no longer fight against those who hate us. But like Dr. King, we will be free to fight for them. And there is a fight to be fought, but it is a different kind of fight, which calls for a different way of fighting.

This is exactly what Paul was talking about in his letter to the church in Ephesus. He outlined for them the kind of weapons they would need for the fight of their lives. He told them to arm themselves with truth, righteousness, peace, faith and the words of Scripture. Clearly, Paul was not planning the normal kind of uprising. He knew the real battle was not against the powers of Rome or against flesh and blood. The real battle is against "the powers of this dark world and against the spiritual forces of evil in the heavenly realms" (Ephesians 6:12).

In other words, if it has a pulse, it is not your enemy.

This is what Dr. King knew. His battle was not against racists but against the dark power of racism. That is why he fought for the liberation of the oppressed *and* the oppressor. The spiritual battle present in our world today demands a different way of seeing the world, and it requires us to see all men and women as image bearers. It asks us to see them as God sees them.

This is the kind of life Jesus calls us into so we can participate with him in bringing the kingdom of God to earth as it is in heaven. This life and this fight invites us to lose it all in order to receive true, lasting freedom. It calls us to pursue what's right, even if we get trampled.

And we will get trampled. People might think we are nervous, sniveling twits. We may be told we are losers and cowards. If we are not willing to play by the rules of the empire, we are going to be kicked to the curb. This business of the kingdom into which we are called to participate is not a way to get ahead in this world—but a way to lose.

In all of this, however, there is a promise: we will inherit the earth. This whole idea sounds nearly impossible, and these ideas would only work in a perfect world. Maybe, but Jesus' teachings were for an imperfect world. Whenever we convince ourselves that taking Jesus literally or living meekly could not possibly work, we are only pointing to the fact that our minds are rooted in the empire's way of thinking, not in the kingdom of heaven's.

We fool ourselves into thinking the empires of the world are the ones in control. With this belief held firmly in our minds, we think that if we are to be a part of God's plan to renew, redeem and restore this world, we must rise to power. So we use the power of the empire for the sake of the kingdom, but this never works. In fact, it has the opposite effect.

The church is at her best not when she has attained power and authority, but in the times when she seeks the highest good of all people—and when, because of her meekness, she gets trampled. The church flourished in the Roman Empire when she was considered a rogue cult. The early Christians were called atheists because they did not believe Caesar was a god. They were burned, maimed, raped, fed to wild animals and crucified. But the church began to wane when Constantine legalized and institutionalized Christianity. Over time, Rome became a Christian nation. Throughout history, when other nations have adopted Christianity as the state-sponsored religion, this has only served to weaken the church. When the church is given political power, it erodes from within.

This was seen during the Crusades. The cross, the ultimate symbol of violence for the Roman Empire, now became the symbol of violence for Christians. They put red crosses on their banners and shields, and they fought beneath the battle cry of Pope Urban II, a leader of the Holy Roman Empire, who said, *"Deus Vult!"* This means, "God wills it." With, they believed, God on their side, the state embarked on a holy war.

This kind of thinking is not just something that happened centuries ago, either. The apartheid regime in South Africa gave Bibles to new military recruits, and told them the Scriptures were their greatest weapon. Eugene de Kock, the captain of the death squads, recalled having Bible studies before he and his men raided villages, killing unarmed men, women and children (Pumla Gobodo-Madikizela, *A Human Being Died That Night*).

In contrast to this, when religious intolerance, persecution and the removal of rights are the reality for a nation, Christianity grows. Throughout church history, in the darkest places, the light shines brightest. In 1950, China became closed to missionaries and Christianity. Estimates reported a million Christians lived in China at that time. Today estimates say 100 million Christians live in China.

I recently met a Christian from Afghanistan. He told me he had to "be secret" in his country just to stay alive but that the church was growing. I asked him how I could pray for him as he returned to his home country. He said, "Pray I would have courage to share my faith, because my country needs the love of Jesus." He was uncertain as to whether he would live or be killed, yet his joy was seeing God's kingdom expand. He was willing to lose it all, because he knew it was never his.

The way of Jesus is a way to lose, be weak and, ultimately, get yourself killed. But we all know what this means, right? That's just the beginning.

Don't get me wrong; we are not to live passively and do nothing. If we simply rolled over and remained silent, we would be overlooked. Those who are meek are not tread upon for doing nothing. The abuse and persecution comes precisely because of what they do in the name of Jesus and for the sake of God's kingdom. They cry out against injustice. They cultivate peace in the midst of war and violence. They defend the cause of the orphan, the widow, the immigrant and all those who are vulnerable.

When I met Angela, mentioned earlier in this chapter, she was fighting, but it wasn't the kind of fight that we see in our world. Her love was more violent than the weakness of bombs and guns. She was not fighting *against* that man who was responsible for his wife's death and sexually assaulted his daughter. Rather she was fighting *for* him because she knew he was not the real enemy. In doing so, she gave him dignity and hope.

We may wonder if we have the resolve to live this way. Because, the truth is, we don't have the resolve or the power to join this fight, but the good news is we do not have to. The power of the resurrection is within us (Romans 8:11). And what happens when the greatest power of death is rendered impotent by the power of God? We become those who are no longer threatened by anything—even by the power of death. If the power of God can beat sin and death, it can certainly smash any barriers that lay inside of us. We become a force, ready for a different kind of fight, and the gates of hell cannot stand against it.

Some of us may still have doubts. That's fine; I know I often do. But there is really only one way to discover the power of the resurrection within us: join the fight. If we have never been in a fight, we will forever wonder about what we are capable of doing. When we join together with God's people and participate with him in the establishment of his kingdom, we will discover the freedom of losing everything to gain more.

The question is left to us. Which way will we choose? Will we choose the way of the empire and continue to wage wars according to its impotent strength? Will we convince ourselves we have to fight, achieve and claw our way to the top? Or will we imitate Jesus? It may cost us everything, but then again, it was not ours to begin with—it was a gift.

15

Closer Than Heaven

Some believe our universe is infinite, but as humans, we do not have the ability to grasp this reality. Yet we still attempt to measure the universe so that we can wrap our minds around how big it really is. But even in our best attempts, there is a limit to how far we can see. The furthest galaxies that have been observed are between ten and twelve billion light years away from us. Scientists suggest that, if there is anything further than that, it might be there, but we won't be able to see it—because our universe has a horizon.

This means that, even when the brightest minds in our world measure the universe, they are only measuring what we can see, which happens to be an area of roughly ninety-three billion light years in diameter. As mind-boggling as this is, some scientists suggest that what we call the universe may only be one small piece of the rest of the universe, which lies beyond our limited horizon.

As big as that is, our universe is expanding and speeding up, which means each galaxy—even those we cannot see—is moving further from us at a faster rate all the time. Just this little bit of information is enough to make your head hurt for days.

The universe that scientists attempt to map—home to trillions of stars, solar systems and planets—which is so unknown and mysterious, is the same place where we may expect to find heaven. We often think of heaven as the place that is "up there." It's somewhere beyond the stars, maybe even beyond the universe. In other words, heaven is not just far from us; it's otherworldly.

With a universe this big, it is no wonder that we often picture God speaking from heaven in a booming voice that sounds like James Earl Jones with a bit of reverb. Thinking like this suggests that God is impossibly far away in his heavenly home. When we conceive of this place as a distant realm, far beyond the horizon of our universe, then what hope do we have of ever reaching him?

The good news is that heaven is not some far-away, distant realm awaiting our postmortem arrival. Heaven is as close as your next breath. Heaven is God's space, intersecting and overlapping, with our space here and now. It's not a place we have to strive to go but a realm, a reality, coming to us.

The writer of Acts tells the story of when Paul went to a place in Athens known as the Areopagus. This was the center of political, religious and philosophical thought. Those present believed in gods who were distant and removed. These gods were so lofty that humans had little hope of ever reaching them.

Paul told the people at the Areopagus about the God of the Bible, who was different than the other gods. He was so close that, if we reached out, we would find him because "he is not far from any one of us" (Acts 17:27). He is not a God beyond the horizon of the universe, stashed away in some blissful heavenly realm. He is here with us. And when we reach out to him, we will find he is already where we are. He always has been.

The Bible speaks of a God who is here in our midst, which means that if heaven is God's space, then heaven may be closer than we could have ever imagined. This is what Jacob, the grandson of Abraham, learned one night as he slept. He laid down on the ground, used a rock as a pillow, fell asleep and had a dream.

In the dream he saw angels, ascending and descending on a ladder, and then saw God himself. God spoke to Jacob and gave to him the same promise he had given to his father, Isaac, and his grandfather, Abraham. When Jacob awoke, he said, "The LORD is in this place, and I was not aware of it" (Genesis 28:16). His language suggests that God had been there the whole time, but Jacob was just waking up to that fact.

This, of course, raises an interesting question: If God had been in that place the whole time and Jacob had just noticed it, then were there other places where God had been where Jacob had missed it? (See Lawrence Kushner, *God Was in This Place & I, I Did Not Know*, p. 27.) Maybe it's the same with us. Heaven is here, in our midst, right now—God is in this place—and, like Jacob, we don't know it.

Jesus had a name for God's space intersecting with ours. He called it the kingdom of heaven. It was the realm of God's rule and reign. It was the space in which God was present and his people were aware of it.

Jesus went around all the time, preaching about the kingdom of heaven, and when he did, the biblical writers said he proclaimed the gospel. Jesus wanted all people to know the renewal of the universe was happening in him and through him. This was his good news. In all of the preaching Jesus did, not once did he speak of getting us out of this world. Rather, he spoke of God's space, or heaven, invading our space. Through this, God will restore our world.

This is why Jesus prayed, "Your kingdom come, your will be done, on earth as it is in heaven" (Matthew 6:10). Jesus' vision was to see heaven and earth once again come back together as they were in the beginning. As humans, we were never meant to get out of here. We were meant to live, thrive and work here on this earth.

What upset this was the power of sin and darkness actively working against God's good creation. When we set our sights on getting off this planet, we run the risk of rejecting the call of God to cocreate and restore his creation with him. We cannot forget that God is working with us to restore, renew and redeem all of creation. All things will be made new, which includes the heavens too.

The prophets spoke of this day. Isaiah wrote about new heavens and a new earth. He was speaking of a new age in which God was once again king. We will live in this reality in the life to come. He wrote the people of God "will build houses and dwell in them; they will plant vineyards and eat their fruit" (Isaiah 65:21).

This is not a disembodied existence. This is a real, material world, made new by the beautiful, endless love and grace of God. The prophet Micah spoke of the day when nations will no longer fight against one another or train for war anymore (Micah 4:3). No more violence and bloodshed. No longer will the highest value of a nation be its own interests or its national security. All people will be at peace.

This vision of the future is not a place to get to but an age God will bring one day when he returns to us and restores all things to himself. This is the time many call heaven. It is a reconciliation of everything, whether things on earth or things in heaven. This happened through the death of Jesus who made "peace through his blood, shed on the cross" (Colossians 1:20).

God, in the person of Jesus, was reclaiming what was his, and we do not have to wait for it all to happen someday. Heaven, God's space, is available and not just after death; we can participate with God in his space now. We can enter the eternal life of heaven today by participating with Jesus in doing the will of God on earth just like it is in heaven. The story of heaven has already begun, and one day will be made complete when God returns to restore all things to himself. This means everything we do in this life matters. Our work is not empty.

This is our joy as God has chosen to use broken, messed up people like you and me to put flesh and blood on the good news of heaven. None of us will do it on our own. But in his power all of us can do our part, and bit by bit, we will see something greater than any of us emerge.

I once visited the massive cathedral in Barcelona called La Sagrada Família. Construction on the cathedral began in 1882 under the inspiration of Antoni Gaudí. When I was there in 1992, scaffolding was all over the place and one of the towering spires was still being built. Today, the cathedral is still unfinished.

Gaudí died in 1926 and never saw his vision anywhere near completion. Thousands have worked on this magnificent structure and have since died, not seeing it completed. Before Gaudí died, he made a powerful statement about the cathedral. He said, "The expiatory church of La Sagrada Família is made by the people and is mirrored in them. It is a work that is in the hands of God and the will of the people" (www.sagradafamilia.cat/sf-eng/docs_instit/historia.php). One begins to wonder if he wasn't talking about heaven.

The kingdom of heaven is a work in the hands of God. In his strength and through his power, heaven and earth will one day be made new. However, we, his people, are the ones who make it a tangible reality for those here on earth.

Whenever we care for the sick, proclaim the hope of Jesus, plant a tree, love our spouse, visit the imprisoned, nurture a child with unconditional love, weep with those who weep, invite others to follow Jesus, provide food for those who are hungry, offer kindness to a stranger, participate in an environmental cleanup, pray for healing, share the gospel of Jesus with a friend, create beautiful works of art, defend the cause of the oppressed, encourage the downtrodden, work faithfully at our jobs or provide clean water for the thirsty, it all matters.

For, in all of those acts, we show others what the kingdom of God looks like—here on this earth, just like it is in heaven. When we are selfless, humble, loving, compassionate, sacrificial, generous, we bring a piece of God's heavenly space to this planet of ours. The more we do this, the more others will come to understand that heaven is not a distant reality in some far-off region of the cosmos.

Heaven is a real presence, here and now, on this earth. For some, this idea is hard to imagine. When we consider the evil many have been forced to endure, it makes sense that some would want to leave this earth; getting out of here and going to a place of bliss in the sky sounds delightful.

This opinion ought not stir defensiveness in us but merely a greater desire to see heaven on earth. Rather than sitting around wanting to escape it all, our response must be to participate with Jesus in bringing his healing and hope to this world. Our sense of urgency to see this happen will never grow until we enter into the existing brokenness in our world.

When the pain and suffering of others becomes ours, we are then in a place to share the hope of Jesus. Rather than tell people how to get out of this place, we have an opportunity to bring a glimpse of heaven into their world and lives.

My friend Ed told a story of three men in Africa who did just this. They decided the best way to be Jesus in their world was to show kindness to another village twenty miles away. The village they chose was a village that they had been at war with for years. The first time they went to this village, they met with the village chief and asked him what his village needed.

This was how they served their neighbors. Every month they met with the village chief, and everything he asked of them, they did. Over the next three years, the neighboring village was so moved by the consistent love of these men that they finally asked what God they worshiped. Through the love of these three men, their neighbors experienced heaven on earth.

Many in the neighboring village entered the kingdom of God. They saw what heaven looked like on earth. Some from that village then chose to go to a neighboring village and serve them. Over time, eight villages were transformed by love. They built roads between these villages that were once fierce enemies, but now they were fellow citizens of the kingdom. Those brothers and sisters were the presence of Jesus in their world.

If this sounds like heaven, perhaps that's because, in some ways, it is. The way of life in these villages in Africa is a picture of the kind of world that once was in Eden. This is what John saw and spoke of in the last two chapters of the book of Revelation. He saw a vision of the future, with a new heaven and a new earth. A voice from heaven said, "Look! God's dwelling place is now among the people, and he will dwell with them" (Revelation 21:3). God came and restored all things to himself. This is how it ends—with God coming to us.

Nothing in those chapters in Revelation speaks about humans ascending up to heaven to float around in the clouds like ghosts. The final verses of the Bible tell the story of God coming and living here on this earth with his people. John saw the city of Jerusalem coming down to earth but saw no temple. Why? "Because the Lord God Almighty and the Lamb are its temple" (Revelation 21:22). Heaven and earth will forever meet in the person of God himself. He will sit on his throne and rule and reign forever. A river will flow from his throne and give life to a garden. It's a picture of Eden, the place called delight.

God remade the heavens and the earth, and brought them back together once again. It is no wonder John says there will be no more death, mourning or crying. And for the tears that are hanging on, our loving God will wipe those away too. We will live in a world where all things are made right. No more will infants live only a few days. There will be no more war. Those who once used weapons of violence will beat those weapons into farm tools. Everyone will sit content under his or her vine or tree. We will be in the place where we see things as they are because they are exactly as they should be.

No more leaves, no more hiding. We will be free to discover the joy of living openly with one another. We will be free to care for and cultivate this new creation God has brought about. We will live, fully known and without shame. We will give and receive love without conditions. We will not have to answer the question, "Where are you?" For God will be with us, and we will be with God at last. We will be found by the one we have been looking for.

Which brings us back to one of the first questions in this book. What if this is true? Not just this part about heaven but all of this?

What if we can stop doing all we can to get to God, because there is a God who is doing all he can to get to us? What if this God is not interested in who others want us to be but only in who he created us to be? What if there is a world where we can be loved for exactly who we are? What if we could step out of the bushes, remove the leaves, and feel God's deep love and warm embrace? What if the one you have searched for all the days of your life is searching for you?

The good news is that we live in light of this reality right now. Heaven is here. God's renewal and restoration of all things has begun, and we are free to reclaim our rightful place on this earth as his people. We are freed from the burden of having to do all we can to get to God, because God is doing all he can to get to us.

He's here waiting, and he is asking, "Where are you?"

So, where are you?

FURTHER READING

On the full extent of the gospel and the cross:
Baker, Mark D., and Joel B Green, eds. *Recovering the Scandal of the Cross.* 2nd ed. Downers Grove, IL: IVP Academic, 2011.
Baker, Mark D., ed. *Proclaiming the Scandal of the Cross.* Grand Rapids: Baker Academic, 2006.

To discover the depth and breadth of the beauty of grace:
Boyle, Gregory. *Tattoos on the Heart.* New York: Free Press, 2011.

The book that started me thinking about God's finding us:
Heschel, Abraham Joshua. *God in Search of Man.* New York: Farrar, Straus and Giroux, 1976.

On God's love for us:
Manning, Brennan. *A Glimpse of Jesus: The Stranger to Self-Hatred.* San Francisco: HarperOne, 2004.

One of the most helpful books I've read about the gospel and salvation:
McKnight, Scot. *The King Jesus Gospel: The Original Good News Revisited.* Grand Rapids: Zondervan, 2011.

To learn more about life as a disciple:
Willard, Dallas. *The Divine Conspiracy: Rediscovering Our Hidden Life in God.* San Francisco: HarperOne, 1998.

Discovering the massively large story of God:
Wright, N. T. *How God Became King.* San Francisco: HarperOne, 2012.

If you'd like to learn how to really fight:
Yoder, John Howard. *The Politics of Jesus.* Grand Rapids: Eerdmans, 1994.